T0322455

This fascinating book is an exploration of resilience in textile art, both in the art itself and in the people creating it, whether an individual maker or a community project. Building on the themes discussed in her earlier bestseller *Slow Stitch*, acclaimed textile artist Claire Wellesley-Smith examines resilience in all its forms, from the enduring fabric creations that have been passed down through the generations to the importance of stitch and textiles in communities today. She explores the historic legacy of the textile industry, particularly in West Yorkshire where she lives, and discusses the relation of textiles to the environment, bringing in ideas about waste, recycling and climate change.

It's packed with mindful practical exercises and ideas to help you explore and develop resilience, using processes such as piecing and patching, making and unmaking, mending and darning, tying and binding, revisiting old pieces of textile work, and dyeing using home-grown natural materials. As well as plenty of stunning examples of the author's own work, the book also showcases pieces based on resilience from some of the world's leading textile artists, including remarkable collaborative work from Alice Kettle made around themes of immigration and the refugee crisis.

The book ends with a poignant postscript outlining one stitch community's response to the 2020 coronavirus pandemic, produced during lockdown. Thoughtful and honest, this captivating book will help you engage with the idea of resilience and find even more meaning in your own textile work.

Resilient Stitch

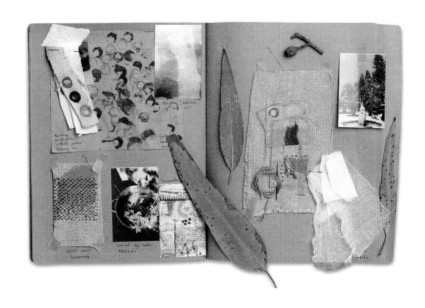

Resilient Stitch

Claire Wellesley-Smith

BATSFORD

First published in the United Kingdom in 2021 by
Batsford
43 Great Ormond Street
London
WC1N 3HZ

Copyright © B.T. Batsford Ltd 2021
Text copyright © Claire Wellesley-Smith 2021

All rights reserved. No part of this publication may be copied, displayed, extracted, reproduced, utilised, stored in a retrieval system or transmitted in any form or by any means, electronic, mechanical or otherwise including but not limited to photocopying, recording, or scanning without the prior written permission of the publishers.

ISBN 978 1 84994 607 0

A CIP catalogue record for this book is available from the British Library.

10 9 8 7 6 5 4

Reproduction by Mission Productions Ltd, Hong Kong
Printed and bound by Toppan Leefung, China

This book can be ordered direct from the publisher at www.batsfordbooks.com

Contents

Introduction

I am an artist and researcher based in the North of England with a practice focused on long-term engagements with communities. These projects use textiles as conversation starters and, through practical and creative activities, as a 'way in' to consider links between mental and physical health, to explore heritage and place, stories of arrival and belonging, and community cohesion. West Yorkshire, where I live, is an area rich in textile heritage and this heritage forms a central part of my working life. I use archives from the industrial production of woollen and cotton textiles that dominated this region to inspire project work and bring stories back into conversation with communities. Recent work has involved exploring the textile-dyeing and recycling industries, looking for and finding stories in the waste, the leftovers, the worn and the discarded. These projects also offer an opportunity to consider the implications of our current relationship with textiles, particularly the challenging issues around the production and consumption of cloth in the 21st century. They offer an opportunity for honest conversations that take place alongside making, remaking and repairing activities with diverse groups of people. My practice has informed the thinking behind this book. In my own work I explore ideas through simple processes that engage with the locations I live and work in. These include a daily stitch practice that embodies my textile and other thinking, and the growing and processing of dye plants to produce local colour on cloth.

Thinking about resilience

Since 2010 I have been interested in the word 'resilience' and how it is applied in many different scenarios, but also its strong link to materiality. My first book *Slow Stitch: Mindful and Contemplative Textile Art* (Batsford, 2015) encouraged taking a thoughtful and meaningful approach to textile practice, using less-is-more techniques and valuing quality over quantity. It explored time as a material and included work by me and other artists that engaged with seasonality and community in the context of ideas from the Slow movement. I hope to extend some of these themes here and consider the importance of connection for individuals and communities when engaging with textiles. Practical ideas around 'thinking through making', using resonant materials and extending the life of pieces using traditional and non-traditional methods are included. Contemporary textile artists consider what the word resilient means to them and share examples from their practice. These feature alongside my own personal work and examples from community-based textile projects.

How to use this book

This book considers resilience, its multiple definitions and uses, and will look at it through materials-based discussion and textile art practices. It is not a project-based book; rather it offers ideas and strategies for considering the materials and processes that might make a 'resilient' textile. Processes include piecing and patching, making and unmaking, mending, tying and binding, revisiting old work and growing colour. I look at resilience through a number of themes: through materials, the environment, history and community. The processes explored are not simply ones that happen when we work on fabric or with other textile activities. Rather they speak of dialogue, with materials and with other people, and in many different communities and settings.

Resilience

Tending to resume the original shape or position after being bent, compressed, or stretched; hard-wearing because of being able to recover after the application of force or pressure.

Of a person, the mind, etc.: tending to recover quickly or easily from misfortune, shock, illness, or the like; buoyant, irrepressible; adaptable, robust, hardy.

Oxford English Dictionary

Resilience is a word that can be defined and used in different ways, mostly in terms of a capacity to recover quickly from difficulties, or to describe a substance or object and its ability to 'spring back' into shape. It is a complex concept and has come to the fore in recent years to describe a number of scenarios. Sometimes used in the context of a societal process, it has also become a process and aspect of research of its own. In policy fields it is used in discussion of diverse issues from climate change, population growth and poverty reduction to urban planning. In healthcare settings it is extensively used in the language around mental health and also preventative action. In self-help books and inspirational mantras, the word often appears. From grassroots campaigning to central government policy, the word 'resilient' crops up time and again. In a time of huge changes in society and the environment there is also the need to process these changes. So perhaps the use of this word in so many contexts is indicative of this need. It is also regularly

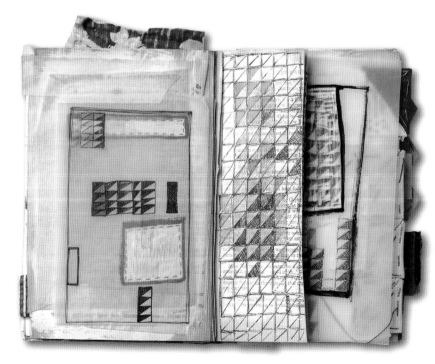

critically appraised, criticized for allowing organizations or underfunded systems using the concept to avoid responsibility, placing the onus on the vulnerable to adapt to difficult situations.

I began to think about the word and its meanings in 2010 while working on a long-term arts and health project that offered participants opportunities to engage with green spaces and creative work. Projects took place in community gardens, mental health organizations and hospitals. Resilience was a word often used in project sessions, where there were conversations around wellbeing, strategies for managing life's complexities, and how a craft practice might help with this. At some stage during this project I made an adapted book using a disintegrating hardback bought at a charity shop. I repurposed it with the word 'Resilience' at its centre, patched textiles and sketches addressing my personal and working life at the time. The book is messy and incomplete, pages painted with gesso to blank out the text, the fabrics used repurposed from baby dresses worn by my young daughters. The adapted book has stayed on the shelf in my studio, sometimes taken out as a teaching sample. It now mainly serves as a reminder of the tenacity of materials and the messiness of life, and as an object with resonance for me. The security of the stitched and bound pages, tied together with handmade string, gather and hold my thoughts from that time.

More recently I have considered ideas of resilience and how they might relate to textiles during an academic research project with The Open University. This looks at how community-based slow craft projects, connected to the heritage of a place, might have an impact on the resilience of the communities based in these areas. Across the North of England, the textile industry, the woollen industry in West Yorkshire where I live and cotton in Lancashire where I often work, remains a feature in the landscape, although much of the industry is now gone. The geography of the areas was a huge influence on the industry being here, the climate and soft water conducive to textile manufacture. The collective industrial work and the processes of working with raw materials, spinning, weaving, dyeing and printing was done by communities that moved for the work, firstly from rural areas to the newly enlarged towns and cities, then from all over the world. These communities have experienced huge changes in the last 40 years, in employment, in income and in health: in many cases deindustrialization has brought with it great disadvantage. My projects in former industrial manufacturing areas involve talking about and making textiles with many people who bring materials-based reminiscences to share. Working with adults in arts and health settings, with intergenerational projects and with those experiencing ill health and disability, has also made me question ideas around resilience.

Above Community quilt being made by participants at the Sukoon-e-Dil group, Roshni Ghar Project in Keighley, West Yorkshire.

Opposite Resilience (2010). Altered discarded book, paper, stitch, recycled textile. 12 × 20 × 4cm (4¾ × 8 × 1½in).

Material

When I first studied textiles, one of the things that fascinated me about the fabrics I was working with, and was beginning to understand, was their flexibility, their stretch. In *On Weaving* the artist Anni Albers describes cloth as 'the pliable plane'[1]. I would take a plain cotton handkerchief square and twist it, pull at the corners, briefly distorting the warp and weft, roll it up, cram it into a ball, pleat it, knot it, gather the points together to carry another object. All of these actions could be performed just using the hands, without need for a pair of scissors or needle and thread, to transform the shape or the potential use. After these interventions, the fabric could be smoothed out by hand again, leaving the square pretty much unaltered. If one changed the fabric composition, to something with stretch or with a looser weave, then this process would create different results. Depending on the flexibility of the fibre, marks of the activity would either be left or not, the fabric usually resilient. Later, as my practice developed, I considered the porosity of cloth, working with large lengths of industrial wool and saturating them with dye. I was interested in how the cloth performed, and how, when dry, it resumed its function.

Above Dyer's Field *(2015). Recycled wool, found dyes. Installation view as part of 'Material Evidence' exhibition at Sunny Bank Mills, Leeds, West Yorkshire. 3 × 1.5m (9¾ × 5ft).*

Opposite Manipulating *a cotton handkerchief to test flexibility.*

I also covered large areas of fabric with multiple stitches that pierced and interrupted the cloth, considering the contraction and manipulation of the surface. Julia Bryan-Wilson, writing in *Fray: Art and Textile Politics* (2017) uses the capacity of textiles to be pulled, stressed, and withstand tension 'sometimes to their breaking point'[2], as a way into a discussion of the tensile properties of textiles, and how this can also connect to the politics of cloth.

When running projects that engaged with stories from the rich textile heritage of Northern England, exploring a period when every fragment of cloth was precious, I also thought about the physical properties of the materials made and used. These projects looked at the impact of industrial textile production: from the miles of cloth emerging from local textile mills to lesser-researched processes, those around the 'end use' of fabric, clothing and fibre. A community engagement project, 'Worn Stories: Material and Memory in Bradford 1880–2015', looked at the histories of textile recycling, repair and reuse in the city, both domestic and industrial. As part of the research for this project I viewed archive samples of fragile textiles, those worn by age, use or sunlight, and rendered brittle, frayed and broken as a result. I also began to collect much-worn samples of cloth and clothing myself, sometimes working them into new objects, sometimes keeping them in their existing precarious state. Their survival seemed miraculous to me, small pieces or garments that could have been so easily lost to time. I see these as resilient objects and that they have the capacity to be made stronger again, through various processes. These could include formal restoration techniques, such as layering with other fabrics, mending using traditional and less traditional techniques, and stitching for reinforcing. Left as they are in their fragile condition, they carry stories of their use, evidenced through threadbare sections, visible darns and other mending. Around the same time, during an artist's residency at Gawthorpe Textiles Collection in Lancashire, I found examples of much-repaired stockings and darned baby bootees among rare collections of silk-embroidered pockets and handmade lace. The collection of Rachel Kay-Shuttleworth offered an interesting and unusual insight into collections of everyday textiles from the local community. These evidence ordinary life and the need of families to preserve their textiles for the longest time possible.

Above *Baby bootees found outside a textile recycling plant in Bradford, West Yorkshire.*

Opposite *Unpicked cotton shirt pocket found as a layer in the interior of a quilt.*

Below *Salvaged unfinished patchwork piece, overdyed with indigo.*

Quilt archaeology

In 2017 antique textile collector and dealer Debs Greensill contacted me offering to send me a gift. A small package arrived in the post containing a smaller package wrapped in tissue paper. Inside was a section of a quilt, unusually thick. A larger piece had been found in a state of considerable disrepair and she had been separating sections that were strong enough to be salvaged for other projects when she sent some to me. Using embroidery scissors, I carefully removed the few remaining quilting stitches anchoring the layers together, and began to explore the interior of the quilt. The top and bottom of the quilt were 1930s glazed cotton floral fabric, and within I counted 17 layers: patched and mended cream blanket pieces with heavily darned sections in a darker coloured wool, folded for additional density; fragments of frayed candlewick bedspread; a filigree of Turkey red-dyed cotton pieced with white, almost worn to nothing; indigo-dyed ticking with red woven stripes. Some of the layers repeated, with selvedge edges and seams from long-dismantled garments, and tiny scraps of print, giving some clues to the age of the pieces. I have used this small section of quilt in object-handling sessions with community groups. It sparks conversations about reuse and repair, about the kind of fabrics used and adapted in the past, about fashions through time, prints, styles, and what might have been in common use. It also has offered an opportunity to talk about need: the use of every tiny scrap, that even those worn beyond repair could still be useful, about construction, and the 'loft' required in a quilt to trap the air within the layers, essential for producing warmth and comfort.

Opposite *Many layers of salvaged fabrics unpicked from a quilt supplied by Debs Greensill.*

Right *A thick section of the salvaged quilt.*

17

Much-vexed Cloths

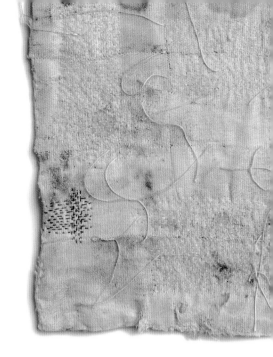

These pieces of work developed alongside a community-based project I coordinated in 2017–19, 'Worn Stories: Material and Memory in Bradford 1880–2015'. This National Lottery Heritage Fund project was delivered for a community arts charity, Hive, and based in many community organizations around the city. The project investigated the heritage of the city's textile recycling businesses and stories connected to the shoddy trade. Normally associated with the area known as the 'heavy woollen district' around Dewsbury and Batley, there was also a smaller industry of this type around Bradford. Today the word 'shoddy' is mostly used as a way of describing something badly made or done, and even something lacking in moral fibre or principle. The original usage is from textile production – that of a material produced from textile mill leftovers and old, used rags. In the early 19th century a process was developed to make recycled and other textile waste into 'new' raw materials in the shoddy towns of West Yorkshire. As part of my own research I read an account from 1860, *A History of the Shoddy-trade* by Samuel Jubb, an industry insider. He describes 'Moth-eaten coats, frowsy jackets, reecky linen, effusive cotton and old worsted stockings'[3] and how they were transformed by machinery known as 'devils' into shredded textile waste, ready to be rewoven into new fabric. His businesses in the heavy woollen district of Yorkshire used recycled pre- and post-consumer textile waste to create new cloth. There are still businesses recycling textiles in this way in the area where I live today, including a large 'shoddy heap' of decomposing textiles.

Left, above and opposite
Much-vexed Cloths *(2018–19). Weathered madder- and indigo-dyed cotton and recycled damask table linen on wool blanket backing, naturally dyed threads, hand stitch. Three pieces 29 × 35cm (11½ × 13¾in), one piece 50 × 50cm (19¾ × 19¾in).*

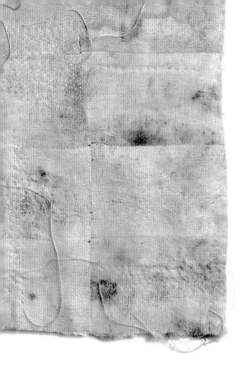

My own *Much-vexed Cloths* are textiles constructed from weathered and much-used cloth: tests for mordant prints, madder-dyed linen, old damask table linen. These were left outside in my back yard for two years to be altered by the elements over time. I often take textiles outside to be weathered; naturally dyed fabrics fade with exposure, making interesting marks and textures. Fibres break down and weaken, meaning that they behave differently when cut and stitched. The printed areas, particularly when iron has been used as a mordant, tend to deteriorate first, leaving patches of weakened and light-faded fabric. This presents challenges and opportunities. I backed these pieces with recycled wool blanket to reinforce them. However, as I began to stitch with silk thread over the weaker areas they continued to fray and to unravel. The more I stitched, the more I needed to repair and make good.

Revisiting old work: interrupted and unresolved

In my studio I have an archive of old work. These pieces are not always completed and include the beginnings of projects that halted due to a lack of time (the needs of family, changing demands of working life, studies) and sometimes through lack of inspiration. I also have a collection of textile pieces that are semi-finished but left in a somewhat open-ended state. These were not planned for exhibition, or for display, but kept, sometimes for many years. Dye tests, print samples, stitched pieces. I consider them interrupted in some way, and unresolved. It is interesting to go back to things years later and look at them with fresh eyes. Has time treated them well? In some cases, their physical appearance may be altered. Much of my work has been made with natural dyes, and depending on the storage conditions some fading may have occurred, but the backs of the pieces will often show the original colour. Fragile, re-used materials patched and pieced together may have degraded, or worse still, been attacked by textile moths. Looking again offers choices. Do I still like them as they are? Is there an impetus to work on them again, adding another layer of narrative to the textile? The piece shown here was begun in 2011, when I was beginning to explore the potential of the common madder plant (*Rubia tinctorum*), using it in community work and also growing and then using my own crop from my allotment.

Madder-dyed sample (2011–19) with mending thread dyed with dyer's chamomile and iron. 14 x 23cm (5½ x 9in).

Above Madder *(Rubia tinctorum) plant grown as part of a community project.*

Opposite Madder-dyed sample (2011–19), *overworked and repaired with stitches using thread dyed with dyer's chamomile flowers.*

Madder has a long heritage as a traditional textile dye and has been used for millennia. I was interested at the time in the process of growing a dyestuff that needs years of cultivation before it can be harvested for colour: the slowness of the process, and the conditions that it took to grow a successful crop. Some of the pieces in this sample were mordanted using an alum-based process and some left un-mordanted before dyeing with fresh madder root. The brightest red areas are on mordanted wool. The fabrics were all reclaimed from a local social-enterprise 'scrap store', including a piece of water-damaged and heavily fulled wool cloth, which picked up the dye unevenly. When coming back to this piece of work I discovered that the areas where I had left pins holding the piece together had rusted the fabric and that this had made it deteriorate. There was also moth damage in one area. After a rest in the freezer (to kill the moth larvae) I looked at it again, deciding to stitch over the damage in a different thread dyed with other local plants. Reinforcing it, working into it anew, creating something else. It speaks of the imperfect, and also of my changing knowledge and understanding of the materials I work with, the colours I can produce and their longevity – methods of reassembling something damaged through repair.

Slow stories or unfinished business

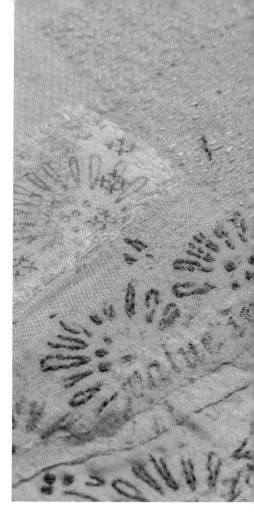

During teaching I have often been asked 'What do I do with all this stuff?' with regard to samples made, often unfinished, during courses and workshops. Some students keep sketchbooks to store these textiles, alongside detailed notes about process. I have found during my own learning experiences that it is easy to build up a collection of pieces of semi-finished work or the beginnings of things, and then leave them in the bottom of a bag, with initial plans to continue working on them but more often than not never touching them again. I have also had conversations with students about excess and the bringing of more 'stuff' into an already overstuffed world; always making more new things rather than focusing on what is already there.

However, looking again at these old samples or pieces of work can offer new opportunities. You can consider them as 'slow stories' and the elapsed time since you last looked at or worked with them can add additional narrative to the work.

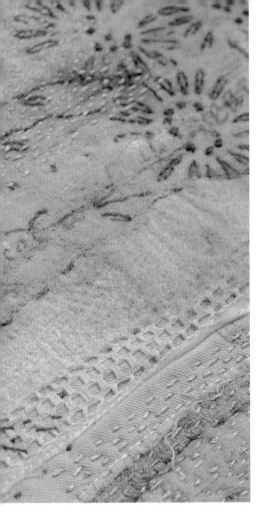

Ask the questions:

- What has moved on for me as a maker since I first made this?
- Has my practice changed, in the materials I use or the processes I engage with?
- What can I add, in skill, in experience, in memories, to these surfaces?
- If the piece had an initial theme, is there something new I want to convey by continuing to work on it?
- Do I want to share this process of transformation or alteration with others?

If the answers to these questions lead you to decide to continue with the work, then you could consider the following ideas for development:

- Re-stitching into the surface. As a hand-stitcher my first instinct is to rework over my existing stitches with new ones. How does it alter the surface? Consolidate the textile? Thicken it, make it bulkier? Is it a comfortable process? Or do the layers of cloth make the surface less easy to handle? Does your choice of stitch affect the feeling of the piece of work?
- Removing a layer or cutting back the surface. Perhaps undoing existing stitches. Does it make it lighter? More malleable and easy to work with again?
- Restructuring and reassembling. Cut it up, reposition pieces, reassemble the whole. In workshops I often encourage students to move their work around on the work surface, turn it 90 degrees and see how this transforms it. Working from the back of an old piece can also have impact.
- Re-dyeing. Compositions made with bright-coloured and patterned fabrics can be unified into a new surface through over-dyeing. Specific textile dyes are not always needed. A strong black tea or one made using coffee grounds can have a surprising way of bringing contrasting fabrics together.

Opposite and above
Value increases with the years *(2006–19), details.*

Above Value increases with the years *(2006–19). Salvaged wool and cotton, iron-on embroidery transfers, hand stitch. 40 × 30cm (15¾ × 12in).*

Opposite *1930s embroidery transfers used in the project.*

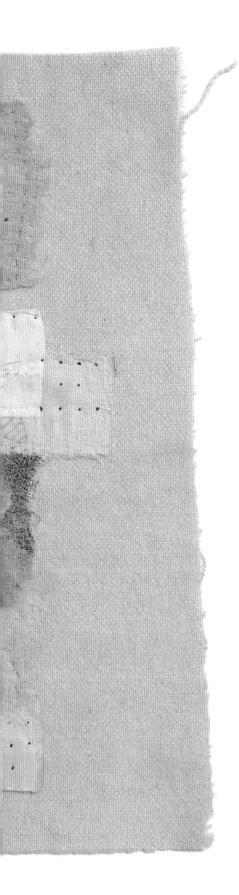

Value increases with the years

Made as part of a series of work in 2006–7, *Value increases with the years* is taken from a line of text found on a second-hand tea towel bought from a charity shop. I was interested in this line in the context of the many textiles I collected at little cost around that time. In second-hand shops and jumble sales, I found textiles made by women, embroidered, tatted, crocheted. The skill and the huge amount of time taken so evident, now discarded and being sold for pence. I cut this piece of text from the tea towel and added it to a wool blanket background with other reused fabrics: the shredded knee area from a pair of my cotton trousers, fragile traditional table linens and rusted scraps of silk. At the time I was also working with text and imagery found in iron-on transfers and had amassed a collection dating from the 1930s onwards. A layer of these, some stitched over and some not, were added to my pieced background. Then, as now, I was interested in accumulations of things, the unused, discarded, and how these speak of time and place. However, at the time, I was unsure about the direction of this piece of work. It was left in a storage box with other samples for over ten years before I revisited it, finding the title intriguing after letting a length of time elapse. I began to stitch over areas of it using old grey silk thread, manufactured at a large local silk mill, erasing some of the content while adding to it.

Amy Meissner

Alaska-based artist Amy Meissner combines traditional handwork, found objects and abandoned textiles to reference the literal, physical and emotional labour of women. Her background is in clothing design, illustration and creative writing, all of which combine in the cloth-based work she began in 2013, initially to address a conflicted mothering experience. Manipulating discarded household cloth to create two-dimensional, quilt-like forms and three-dimensional objects serves as a cultural nod to the embroidery created by generations of Scandinavian women in her family, and confronts societal disregard and erasure of women's handwork.

Amy's work is traditional, fine and craft-based, relying on the repetitive nature of hand-stitching to relay a manic and confrontational feminist subject matter. The work is approachable and tangible, its components even familiar, but challenges the viewer's emotional history to convey layered messaging around femininity, motherhood and the value of women's labour. This is time-based work, using old skills. An act of cutting apart, then piecing oneself back together.

Amy writes, 'I approach resilience in my work through the lens of a woman and mother, always pointed towards the intersection of the literal, physical and emotional work of women. I consider sustainability, mostly through material choice, but also through maintaining a traditional set of women's handwork techniques. Resilience, for me, is connected to adaptability, so as an artist I'm constantly questioning my work: how do I best pursue a resilient and sustainable practice? How do I engage with my own emotional resiliency in order to convey a narrative? How do I extend the life of fugitive materials? Why do this work and what needs to shift? As someone committed to a craft-based practice, I value the history and material culture of women's needlework. The fact that it persists, despite being traditionally marginalized, relegated to "low" or "minor art," is a testament to its

Above right Amy Meissner (USA), War Room *(2017), detail. Vintage baby quilts, abandoned embroidery and domestic and household linens, upholstery foam, tapestry needles. 116 × 157 × 7cm (45½ × 61¾ × 2¾in).*

Right Amy Meissner (USA), Shadow Self *(2019). Abandoned and unfinished embroideries, household linens, cotton embroidery, wool. 182 × 167cm (71¾ × 65¾in).*

ability to persevere. We will always be mothers, sisters, grandmothers; we will always pass these skills on, and through the act will honour the hands and bodies of those who came before us.'

War Room considers the domestic landscape of the home, the bed, children and family relationships, using the template of an old-fashioned war room paradigm. The troop manoeuvres wander aimlessly in this context, battle scenes become meaningless, but the conflict in this environment is just as tangible.

Amy Meissner goes on to say that as a girl, embroidery lessons emphasized repetition and perfection, the reverse always finished as finely as the front. This tradition of teaching young women handwork skills readied them for society's expectation of womanhood and motherhood, teaching patience, tidiness, domestic skills, cleanliness, silence. Their finished work was meant to be a reflection of themselves and their households. Instead, *Shadow Self* reveals a messy reverse side, a thread-skipping, knotted underbelly never meant to be seen. From the point of view of the woman who chose not to have children, the piece asks: 'Who would I have been as a mother?' From the voice of the mother, it's the darker question: 'What if I'd never had children at all?'

Making and unmaking

I remember my mother laying layers of old cloth, five maybe, on the
floor and smoothing them out for stitching sheets, quilts, wrappings.
Participant, Sukoon-e-Dil group, Roshni Ghar Project

In my collection of old and used textiles there are examples of
items that exist because of other items. The battered quilt section
that incorporated women's dress pieces as layers, evident from
the pocket and placket found inside. Countless sections of English
paper-pieced patchwork, incomplete, unfinished and with papers
still inside assembled from years of collections of family textiles,
or, for wealthier women, including chosen fabric purchased for the
purpose so that print and pattern matched.

I was also recently the recipient of a broken section of kantha
quilt, thick but now disintegrating, with more recent mending in
brighter and more contemporary fabrics alongside softer layers of
worn, repurposed, light-faded cotton. This was a functional *dorokha*
kantha, where layered pieces of worn cloth (usually patterned
lungis or sarongs) were stitched together using simple running
stitch to make a two-sided quilt. The technique originated in Indian
Bengal, now Bangladesh. The sides of the cloth would be tacked
together to stabilize the work and running stitch added to hold
the pieces together, the join between different cloth and patterns
hidden. I have other examples on beds and sofas in my house used
as everyday textiles, but due to its condition this example was not
suitable for reuse in the conventional sense. It offered, though, an
opportunity to examine its making through an unmaking process. I
was interested, after looking at the quilt sample with 17 layers (see
page 17), in how much fabric had gone into this kantha, and the
physical work required to sandwich the layers together with thick
white cotton thread.

Mid-20th-century cotton kantha, collection of the author.
140 × 170cm (55 × 67in).

Artist Helen Carnac says, 'The making and unmaking processes that take place in order to do this involve a layering of knowledge and sensibility in the handling of material that develops through time spent, and an appreciation of changing technologies over time'.[4] In recent teaching sessions I asked participants to consider then unpick a small section of the broken kantha quilt using an unpicker or small embroidery scissors. In the spirit of process I was interested in what happens when you spend time 'unmaking' something as a way of considering its form and structure and also how the layers of construction can tell a story. The responses by the groups were interesting. A couple of students demurred from the task, feeling it inappropriate to undo the labour of other women. For others unpicking the densely stitched layers proved physically difficult. One participant commented '... unmaking is hard work. These are very solid stitches.' As a group we also decided that your understanding of a textile is different if you unmake it, as you understand more

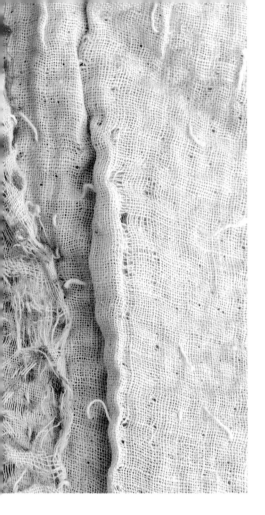

Opposite and above Fine
cotton layers unpicked
from a kantha, with
needle marks visible.

Above right Patching on
patching: the kantha as
a process of making and
remaking.

the work that went into making it. 'You have a better connection to
the person that made it' was one comment, and 'I felt the need to
be careful and methodical to give regard to the people who made
it. I feel like I'm marking them in some way.' Unmaking a textile
transforms it in a new way, and through that it also presents an
opportunity. The layers of the kantha when unpicked showed the
marks of the needle as it pierced multiple layers of cloth leaving fine
cotton fabrics with a punctured filigree of patterns running through
them. As Jennifer Higgie comments in 'Thoughts on Making and
Unmaking' (2018) an essay accompanying an exhibition curated
by Duro Olowu, 'Materials have their own (often oblique and ever-
changing) logic, one that allows for constant rediscovery. The thrill
of making lies in the possibility of what might be unearthed, both in
the maker and in the materials.'[5]

Sampling and remaking

I like to reconstruct old fragments of textile as samples – sometimes developed into bigger pieces of work, but sometimes used as another way of 'thinking through' the textile and considering its previous use and owners. The sampling begins with one fabric and I build other choices around this, perhaps based on a feeling, on a theme, or on other textiles in my collection.

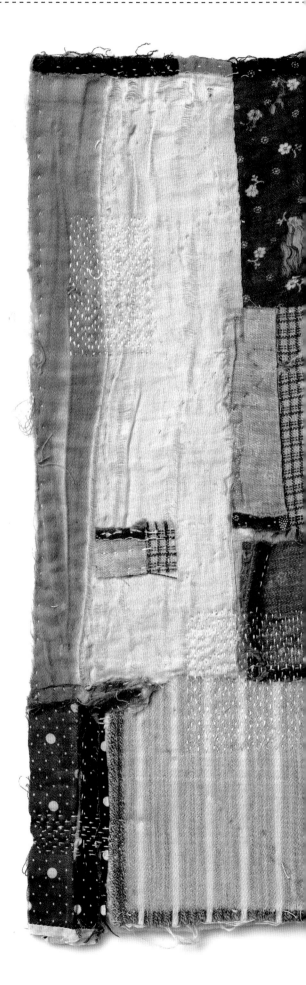

Above Unpicked fabric from an indigo cotton quilt, with stitch marks visible due to light-fading.

Right Reconstructed sample using fabric from deconstructed cotton quilts, hand stitch, silk thread on wool background. 50 × 25cm (19¾ × 9¾in).

Materials

- *Scissors, needle of choice and a pincushion.*
- *Frixion or other textile marking pen, small templates in different shapes.*
- *Small pieces of fabric including patterned, neutral and plain. I often include fragments of old quilts, shirts and hand-dyed fabrics that speak of the plant and the place they came from, and look for soft and pliable fabrics that will be pleasing to re-work.*
- *Another piece of repurposed cloth as a background. Choose something with some stability but not so thick that hand-stitching will be a struggle. My preferred way of working is into a piece of old woollen blanket as I like the solidity of the new constructed fabric when stitched on top. Quilt wadding or cotton domet, or a few layers of a thinner fabric, would also work well.*
- *A contrasting coloured thread for tacking your fabric pieces onto the background.*
- *A neutral-coloured sewing cotton – pale beige works well. Neutral thread blends well when using multi-coloured or patterned fabric compositions.*
- *Threads of your choice for topstitching. These could be traditional stranded cotton embroidery threads, split into two or three for ease of stitching. I like to include some of my own plant-dyed silk or bamboo thread (there is a tutorial describing a method for this in* Slow Stitch) *but often use ordinary sewing thread.*

Method

1. Choose one fabric to build your composition around. It might not be that this becomes the biggest piece, or the most visible, but it is a good way to begin. Lay it on your base fabric.

2. Choose another four fabrics to work with. I usually include a neutral fabric as part of this as my preference is to have some negative space in compositions. This is often a neutral linen, unpicked and reused from charity shop shirts and trousers. Pick one fabric that has a contrast, something that is bright or a piece of pattern. It helps to draw the eye and provides a focal point.

3. Visual clutter can be confusing when working through ideas so clear your workspace, just leaving the fabrics and backing fabric, a pair of scissors and a pincushion.

4. Play with your fabrics, moving them around on the base fabric. Pin them down and tape them to a wall so that you can stand back and see them from a different point of view. Consider what makes the assemblage interesting to you.

5. When you are happy with your layout, tack your fabrics to the surface and iron.

6. You can work over the tacked stitches, securing them invisibly with the neutral thread, and then choosing an area to work in heavier, more concentrated hand stitch.

7. Mark an area centrally on your composition using your marking pen and a template. You could also draw an area freehand.

8. Use a thread of choice to apply dense stitches to the marked area and then add additional stitches to the surface.

Samples using scrap fabrics showing, from top left, the process of marking and stitching.

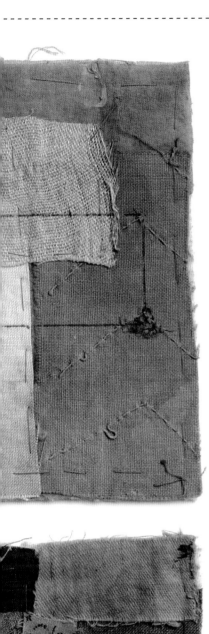

Lynn Setterington

Lynn Setterington is based in the UK, where her quilts and cloths are held in collections including the V&A, Crafts Council and the Whitworth Art Gallery. Her work uses stitch to commemorate people and communities and explores contemporary issues and the everyday. Lynn writes:

Hand embroidery opens up dialogical exchange and is a form of communication even without words. It encourages resilience and strength and is a way of drawing people together, especially women.

My early work celebrates the everyday and the reverie of objects, depicting domestic artefacts and rituals in meticulously worked quilts and embroideries. The link to kantha quilting goes back many years and I was the first British maker to adopt this approach in the late 1980s. It led to a wide range of stitch-based collaborations with women from the South Asian diaspora, something that has continued sporadically ever since.

Dulwich Mum (2016) depicts a ubiquitous supermarket shopping trolley and the colours and motif reflect those of the supermarket Lidl. The title refers to an incident which made the news in 2008 – a woman from affluent Dulwich was spotted with Lidl shopping bags. The artwork highlights snobbery in the press, and how shopping habits have changed over the last ten years, in that middle-class shoppers visiting cut price supermarkets is now commonplace.

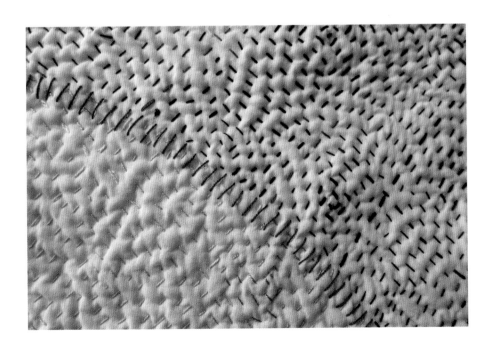

Opposite Lynn Setterington (UK), Dulwich Mum *(2016); detail shown left. Cotton and cotton perle thread, Cornely embroidery and hand stitch. 96 × 98cm (37¾ × 38½in).*

Community

Over many years my community-based practice has largely consisted of projects that use textiles in some way. This could be through a story from the local textile heritage, through practical techniques learned and shared, or by exploring the emotional resonance of textiles through reminiscing projects. The development of community projects is a long process of learning alongside new people, sometimes from different cultures and with multiple languages. There is a sense, as a practitioner, of being an outsider in these settings, and of needing to find common ways of communication, not always verbal. Often, I have found a textile activity offers a space of cooperation, for collaboration and potentially for increased wellbeing. Sometimes projects are designed to be co-created, where an idea is developed by a group of people who share skills, knowledge and ideas. A shared stitch, a conversation that happens through the passing around of a piece of cloth and exploring its construction, its use and its history can be convivial. It can also offer ways of exploring commonalities.

There is an increasing body of research into arts-based activities and their role in wellbeing. The last decade has seen an increased awareness of the impact wellbeing has on our overall health and how this works in living, working and learning environments. In projects I often use the definition provided by The New Economics Foundation (2007) of wellbeing as 'feeling good and functioning well.'[6] Increasingly there is an interest in how government policy can have more of a focus on wellbeing outcomes. Alongside this interest is academic research that measures wellbeing in a variety of ways. A growing evidence base is demonstrating the significant impact of arts and culture on individual and collective health and wellbeing. A 2019 World Health Organization report that looked at over 3,000 arts-based interventions and reports from around the world concluded that the contribution of the arts to the promotion of good health and the prevention of other mental and physical health conditions was evident.

Opposite *Community cohesion event at Hive, a community arts charity in Bradford, West Yorkshire, working with recycled fabric and print. Artists Claire Wellesley-Smith and Claire Rookes (2018).*

Groups based in arts and health environments may include participants who have experienced great difficulty in their lives, through mental or physical ill health, personal loss or bereavement, social isolation and loneliness. My experience of this kind of work shows that a textile craft element can offer a way to participate quietly and alongside others. A participant on a textile heritage project offered this insight: 'I've learned that you don't have to do a lot of talking. Just listening to people's ideas can help you. Even if you sit quietly you can learn such a lot.' Weiner and Schneider write in *Cloth and Human Experience* that 'Another characteristic of cloth, which enhances its social and political roles, is how readily its appearance and that of its constituent fibres can evolve ideas of connectedness or tying.'[7] Cloth can be celebratory, bringing colour and conversation to projects where there is a common goal, and offers ways to share skills and an end outcome. It can act as a linking structure, building friendships and relationships. In this section I share ideas around community, the materials that can tell stories of communities, and the potential of projects to craft community resilience.

The community scrap-bag

My community-based practice moves around the former textile cities and towns of northern England. I follow threads through the fragmentary remains of a once huge industry: tracing, connecting, weaving together memory through the exploration of places, communities, people. I often work on multiple projects at the same time and these are based in community settings around the region. I drive from venue to venue with a car boot full of equipment, ironing board, boxes of scissors, collections of threads, materials for use during project sessions.

My 'kit' includes a scrap bag: a jute sack stencilled 'Java Coffee Brazil', once full of coffee beans. It is full of textile scraps, collected over years of community-based projects and teaching. Remnants, discarded clothing, donations from local shops and markets, gifts from craft hobbyists, leftovers from previous collaborative projects. The contents of the bag undergo occasional edits, mostly due to it becoming too unwieldy when carrying it from car to venue and back again. When I edit the contents, I tend to reduce bulk by cutting up larger pieces of fabric, so the contents remain unaltered other than the size of the cloth. The scrap bag has become an informal working archive of sorts, documenting histories of use, the generosity of individuals and communities, and the possible generative processes to come. It is not ordered in any way but as one of the tools of my trade I differentiate, categorize and remember as I sift through the contents: the people, objects, garments deconstructed to provide new raw material for collaborative projects.

Right and opposite
My community scrap bag,
a recycled coffee sack.

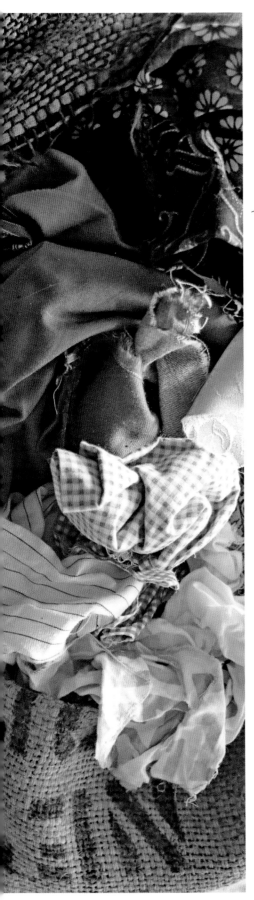

A handful of cloth pulled from the bag provides me with the following:

- A man's shirt sleeve, white background, pale blue pinstripes, slightly worn at the elbow.
- Silky, synthetic white machine-embroidered edge strip with gold sequins from a shalwar kameez. This arrived in a bin liner full of similar edges, hems and trims donated by a dressmaker from the local Bangladeshi community.
- Red gingham polycotton, overlocked edges, from a summer school uniform dress.
- Worsted wool offcut with 'Made in England' woven into the selvedge.
- White cotton lawn sari, with a woven brown border. Soft through washing and use.
- A scrap of madras cotton in blue and green checks from a child's shirt.
- Mustard-coloured polycotton. Part of a large collection of fents (remnants) from a local market donated for a community quilt.

The diversity of these fragments allows for a moment of textile thinking, and there are many stories gathered in the bag. The participants in projects and individuals who come to my workshops have informally curated the contents of the scrap bag. It contains a mixture of mostly old and some new fabrics and fibres – textile debris of sorts. I am interested in the other stories present: the traces of garment makers, of bodies within clothing: the actions performed on the fabrics, sorting, folding, washing, ironing are in the bag too. My own knowledge, of the provenance of the materials in the bag, is something I often share as I embark on new teaching, or new processes with groups using the contents. When groups from different areas or parts of the city get together for project activities, they also share stories about the materials they have chosen to use. As Gregson and Crewe describe, 'Second hand goods are imbued with a history and a geography and, theoretically, all the things of material culture have the potential to become meaningful, even when they have been effectively withdrawn and deactivated as commodities through, for example, disposal, damage, or decay.'[8] To the imaginative potential of the former life of these materials is added the generative possibilities of them as reinvented 'new' materials for use in craft-based processes.

The materials in the community scrap bag have been transformed into many things over the years. Patchwork in many forms, including a community banner made at a project for refugee and asylum seekers' families; many, many pincushions; balls and dolls. The balls were made of fabrics wrapped and tied with sewing thread, part of a reminiscing project with older women from the South Asian community where they demonstrated traditional toy-making and games they played with them as children. In another project, strips of fabric cut from T-shirts created yarn for weaving, knitting, crochet and macramé, and were later transformed into baskets, bags and plant holders. Plain and patterned fabric from the scrap bag was overdyed with indigo at a community dye workshop to unify the surface and the pieces then used in patchwork.

Toy balls made from scrap fabric wound with sewing thread. Sukoon-e-Dil group, Roshni Ghar Project, Keighley, West Yorkshire.

Tying and binding:
scrap string

Thinking of ideas of tying and binding in the context of communities, I used some of the fabric from the community scrap bag to make fabric string. This is a simple method and the resulting fabric can be used in many ways. It is strong enough to use in gardens to tie up plants, I have used it to tie bundles of fabric and documents in my studio, and for couching to another surface. It is also a useful visual way of condensing a fabric collection into one single piece of yarn: amalgamating it as an object to think about, a collaborative exercise with a group, or simply for practical use. It is a good way of using up any sort of scrap fabric, but works particularly well with fabrics with a high percentage of cotton.

Opposite Making string from scrap fabric can be a collaborative activity.

Below Scrap string made using cotton and polycotton fabrics.

Method

1. Cut scrap fabric into strips 2cm (¾in) wide and any length.

2. Take two strips and knot them together at the ends.

3. Hold the knotted join with one hand, and with the other twist the top strip of fabric away from you tightly four or five times.

4. Pull the twisted strip over the second strip, continuing to twist. The twisting action keeps the twine in place and when you let go will continue to 'grab' the second strip, keeping it from unravelling.

5. Repeat, making sure you keep twisting away from you.

6. When you come to around 5cm (2in) from the end of a strip of fabric you need to join the next piece.

7. Wrap the next strip of fabric inside the existing strip and continue to twist.

Opposite and below
Machine-pieced scraps can also be used as one of the fabric strips for twining. This method can use up even the smallest scrap.

Tattered Lives

Tattered Lives was made by women's community groups in Bradford in 2018 as part of a textile heritage project, 'Worn Stories: Material and Memory in Bradford 1880–2015'. A two-year project (2017–19), it was coordinated by me for Hive, a community arts charity, and funded by the National Lottery Heritage fund. Hive has worked across Bradford in community settings for over 35 years in the arts and health/wellbeing field. The project was devised to look at the history of textile repurposing and recycling in the city at a time when there was much debate about the textile and clothing industry and its sustainability. The project offered volunteers and participants the opportunity to take part in a variety of activities and learning. These included training in research skills and oral history interviewing. In community settings around the city, including mental health organizations, refugee and asylum seeker groups and intergenerational projects, creative textile workshops explored traditional textile recycling and reuse techniques. The project also offered opportunities for personal reminiscing and sharing about the value of textiles, their use and disposal in our everyday lives. An exhibition of community-made textiles, interpretation of research, photographs and archive objects was shown at Bradford Industrial Museum between November 2018 and March 2019, where a symposium about the themes of the project was also delivered.

Tattered Lives is the collective work of 40 project volunteers. It features the stitched names of 160 female rag workers and sorters identified by research project volunteers in a 'creed register' held by West Yorkshire Archives. These registers listed the personal details and circumstances of people on entry to the workhouse. The jobs the rag workers did included sorting and grading rags by fabric type, colour, quality and state of disrepair, sometimes into as many as 30 different categories. The women discovered by the project entered Bradford Union Workhouse between 1898 and 1915, partly due to the precarious nature of the work and its poor pay in this part of the Bradford textile industry. Their names were stitched onto reclaimed wool fabric donated by local industry partners including Hield Brothers Ltd and Randisi Textile Recycling Ltd. In community sessions, as the names were stitched, we explored stories from these women's lives using the biographical details that emerged

from the research. Annie Elizabeth Uttley, b.1889, who had three daughters, one of whom died in infancy in the workhouse; Bridget Needham, b.1841, widowed before entering the workhouse; Margaret Mullarkey, who organized a protest against the poor quality of workhouse food that was reported in the local press. The stories of these ordinary working-class women had been untold before now. Conversations in the group sessions drew on the experience of women working together, whether in industry or community, stories connected by the red thread chosen by participants to stitch the letters.

As I am stitching her name I am thinking about the things we may have had in common. It's like a conversation across the centuries.
Project participant

Left and above Hive
Talking Textiles Group
(UK), Tattered Lives *(2018).*
Pre- and post-consumer
wool waste, cotton thread,
cotton tape, hand stitch.
35m (115ft) × various
lengths.

Lynda Steele, one of the participants in this project, reflected on her experience of stitching in a group:

The drop-in group met up weekly at the local community arts centre. There was a friendly, relaxed atmosphere, and we all got along okay, but we seemed to be a bunch of individuals, slightly detached and mainly speaking to the person sat next to us. The 'Worn Stories' project interested us all but I was expecting the essential character of the group to remain the same; a bit disparate, separate people, not really bound together. But the ethos changed quite quickly and developed into something genuine with meaningful connections. This change sort of crept up on us, whilst we were stitching, our hands holding onto cloth and needles, and chatting about historical lives. We were gently gaining confidence and trust in our own lives, sharing experiences, some poignant and difficult to express, but we learned that we all shared similar stories, and a natural empathy grew among us, which reflected in the often difficult lives of the women we were studying.

The focus always came back to our hands; grounding us in the comfort of repetitive stitching, engaged with our creative task. For me, this seemed to dilute my anxiety about engaging with others and give a sense of proportion to what I was feeling. This led to glimmers of resilience – which took me by surprise.

Pulling a strand of red thread through a piece of grey blanket and discussing which stitch to use, or having a feel of some strange shoddy cloth and exchanging opinions on it, could appear to be very ordinary little social exchanges, but to the socially isolated they hold significance, and are a bit extraordinary.

I think that small community groups fulfil a vital role in reducing social isolation and prejudice. Mental wellness can be gained from engaging with like-minded creative people, feeling included and having the opportunity to chat and share. Experience has taught me that when these basic requirements are lacking, mental ill health can quickly develop, and the distress this causes can be major.

On the last day of the project, a lot of women felt confident enough to address the whole group, and it had grown into a big group, to say how they felt about being part of the project. It was extremely moving to hear what a positive difference to their wellbeing it had made. Combined with the textile tasks, we had felt listened to, and accepted in a unique way. The experience has given us a stronger sense of self. The two hours we spent together each week radiated out much further into my life, I felt part of something in my community, and therefore part of my community.

Above 'Worn Stories: Material and Memory in Bradford 1880–2015'. *Exhibition image, Bradford Industrial Museum, 2018. Top,* Tattered Lives *exhibit; below, work on reclaimed wool blankets by members of the Hive Talking Textiles Group. Artists, clockwise from top left: Ann Colley (just seen), Lynda Steele, Lila Jovanovich, Susan Oliver, Muriel Driver.*

Angela Maddock

Angela Maddock is an independent academic and artist. Her work primarily explores how the methodologies of textile practice contribute to healthcare education. She held a Parallel Practices Award from the Crafts Council and King's College, London from 2016–17. She continues to work with the Faculty of Nursing, Midwifery and Palliative Care at King's, and also contributes to Clinical Humanities teaching with medical students. Angela is interested in how transforming materials enables reflective thinking across disciplines and particularly how our shared experience of cloth and threads facilitates new knowledge. 'I like to describe myself as being bothered by cloth, which means that I am very invested in what cloth means to me, what it feels like next to my skin, how it is made and unmade and how it is central to our lives, whether or not we are even aware of this.'

I asked Angela to tell me about her thoughts on resilience:

> Materially, resilience is often described as being like rubber, and someone who is resilient has the capacity to bounce back after a particularly difficult or testing time. I do not enjoy this analogy. Instead, I prefer to employ ideas of porosity and stretch when considering resilience, and often use the metaphor of the perfect-fitting knitted garment, one that is capable of stretch, of give and take, and yet returns to its original form – if well treated. Being porous is important, it speaks of empathy and does not carry with it the solid outer exterior of thick skin, of rubber. I often use Kozloff's writing on softness to support this, 'an object that gives in is actually stronger than one that resists, because it also permits the opportunity to be oneself in a new way.'[9] I find that nursing and midwifery students respond well to thinking of resilience in this way, it enables some agency, particularly around the question of 'How do I look after myself?'

Left Angela Maddock and the Midwifery Quilting Bee (UK), Being Intimate (2017–ongoing), detail. Deconstructed and reconstructed undergarments of various materials, stitched with mercerized sewing thread and embroidery floss.

One common error is to confuse resilience with grit; this returns me to Kozloff. Grit can only sustain in the short-term, get you through a stressful shift or a particularly testing trauma. Grit wears away at fibres, so that perfect knit will be stressed by grit, worn through even, leaving holes that must be darned; a knit is better hand-washed than put through the mangle. A mental health nursing lecturer described resilience as something that ought to be prophylactic (an interesting turn on rubber!), in that it needs to be proactive rather than reactive, otherwise we start talking of burnout. This is important.

Resilience is a tricky concept, but not to raise it, not to work with it or on it, is a mistake. We need a discourse on resilience that challenges its appropriation by a neo-liberal agenda, one that engages with materiality and one that considers its construction, its very making.

The paediatrician and child therapist D. W. Winnicott described the phenomenon of the 'good-enough mother'[10]. I would like to think of resilience as somehow adopting Winnicott's ambition to be 'good enough', to accept our imperfections and occasional failings. Such ambition sits uneasily in healthcare provision, where occasional flaws and failings, whilst often human, can also be life-changing.

Angela Maddock and the Midwifery Quilting Bee (UK), Being Intimate *(2017–ongoing). Deconstructed and reconstructed undergarments of various materials, stitched with mercerized sewing thread and embroidery floss. 230 × 110cm (90½ × 43¼in).*

Being Intimate:
the midwifery quilting bee

This quilt began in 2017 as an exploration of intimacy with midwifery students and staff. I wanted us to explore what a woman might have to give of herself during pregnancy, delivery and the post-natal period. The head of midwifery supported the project, which included teaching staff and students. We worked with our underwear, all worn yet clean. Favourite pants, knickers and a pair of boxer shorts belonging to the only male student. Displays of wished-for, long-forgotten and literal stains, the leaking body. We unpicked them, 3D transformed into 2D, and re-pieced them. All of us mingled together – cotton, silk, polyester, elastic – a proper crazy quilt, and a complete collapsing of hierarchies. All the time we chatted in the manner of what I've come to think of as sideways talking. Discussion that often began at the material level, 'how soft this feels', 'how difficult this is to unravel' and soon moved into deeper territory, the impact of observing a particularly traumatic emergency caesarean section on a first labour ward placement, anxieties around learning to perform episiotomy repairs.

From winter through to summer we met, unpicked, stitched, chatted, worked it – and sometimes us – out, slowly. The backing cloth, an unpicked student uniform, and all our names stitched at the centre, the space created by the separation of the trouser legs – a symmetry of sorts. It was displayed at the Festival of Quilts in 2017, the group's male midwife bearing witness.

But it is a tricky thing, this quilt made of underwear; laughable, embarrassing, amateurish.

This reconstitution of eight different bodies into one also occurs at a site whose most immediate referent is to another intimate space, the bed[11] and threatens to tip the whole thing into the obscene. Perhaps, not wholly unsurprisingly, it has still to find a permanent home on the faculty walls. Yet it has a very clear purpose: its legacy. It remains an unfinished thing, regularly used with seminar groups, at the transition between year one and two, at the beginning of the third-year arts and humanities module, at the International Day of the Midwife. Its continuing openness offering a way in, to come 'to the table', to share thoughts and ideas, find someone who might listen. Find an unmarked corner, trace a thread, leave a mark, bring the singular into dialogue with the multiple.

Improvised backgrounds from textile waste

This is a method of using up scraps and sometimes finding surprising and challenging compositions. It comes from my experience of working on community-based projects that address textile waste and scarcity in their subject matter, and often have small budgets for materials. There is also a sense of creating a community fabric when using cloth accumulated by many different people and amalgamating it in a new way. In teaching I have used this method to challenge students to consider what happens when you 'use what you have' in a completely improvised way. Removing choice and then working with what you have can be both freeing and slightly terrifying, and has been received in both ways by students. It could also be used as a 'warming up' exercise on days when it is difficult to know where to begin with a textile project. As a community or group project it could produce the background to a collaborative piece of work, participants encouraged to all contribute something to the mix.

The samples shown included chambray denim from a child's dress, a printed cotton velvet recycled from a skirt, patterned cotton dress fabric, sari silk and two plain cottons. The blends of fabric, plain, patterned, their handle silky, smooth, textured and different weights, when simply pieced together by hand or with a sewing machine create starting points for me.

Materials

- *3 paper bags*
- *Scissors (or rotary cutter, cutting mat and ruler)*
- *Iron and ironing surface*
- *Hand-sewing needle (or sewing machine)*
- *Scraps of 5 fabrics in different sizes collected randomly from your scrap collection. Do not limit yourself to offcuts. You could also include sampling from other projects, discarded clothes, etc.*

Right Paper bags of scrap fabrics for improvised backgrounds.

58

Method

1. This process works best with smaller pieces of fabric, but to introduce more structure in the piecing, first separate your fabrics into small, medium and larger pieces before putting them in paper bags: 1 (large), 2 (medium) and 3 (small).

2. Take a piece of fabric from your paper bag 1 of larger scrap pieces, trim it to a rough square or rectangle shape and iron it. Try not to look when pulling the fabric from the bag.

3. Take a piece from paper bag 2 and place it on the side of your first piece, right sides together, and stitch with a 1cm (½in) seam; use backstitch if hand-stitching. Iron flat.

4. Take a piece from paper bag 3 and add to the composition in the same way.

5. Continue to add scraps from each paper bag, rotating the newly assembled piece of fabric and ironing as you go.

6. Trim the edges of the block. These edges will now contain ready-made pieced strips, that can be added to your next composition.

7. You can experiment with sizes and with structures. In the examples shown, some compositions are linear, others constructed like a quilt block.

Building on your experimental block

Tape the assembled block to a wall or board so you can look at it from a distance. Does it appeal? Consider how it might look as part of another assemblage:

- Added to neutral fabric.
- As a surface for other stitches.
- As a prompt for unexpected combinations.
- As a story-making object, using the provenance of the materials as a starting point.
- If working with a group try amalgamating the blocks into a single piece of fabric.

Environment

Communities today across the globe are experiencing environmental and social transition. Population growth, migration and globalization are having a huge impact on the resilience of communities. Carbon emissions, loss of bio-diversity and large-scale environmental pollution associated with consumerism are all contributing to climate change. This impact on the natural and built environments has seen such fast change that it is sometimes hard to find the words to explain, understand and comprehend it. Philosopher Glenn Albrecht, looking for language to describe the anxiety and loss connected with this change uses the word 'solastalgia' to describe the emotional or existential distress caused by environmental change. 'Solace has meanings connected to the alleviation of distress or to the provision of comfort or consolation in the face of distressing events. Desolation has meanings connected to abandonment and loneliness. The suffix -algia has connotations of pain or suffering. Hence, solastalgia is a form of "homesickness" like that experienced with traditionally defined nostalgia, except that the victim has not left their home or home environment.'[12]

Community-based arts engagement and individual studio practices have the opportunity to address some of these issues on a human-sized scale. This can be through a conscious use and sourcing of materials: local sourcing, reusing and recycling. Arts engagement and activity can provide an opportunity for participants and audiences to have conversations, offer solutions, see connections, offer a collective response. Creative projects can also offer an opportunity to see how small change at individual and local level can make a difference. Working this way can encourage hope and counter anxiety.

Opposite, above Making connections through stitching in multiple languages and sharing hopes for the future at a community project for Refugee Week, June 2018.

Opposite, below Plant life beginning to return after fire destroyed its habitat on Ilkley Moor, West Yorkshire.

Growing resilience

I have worked on many community-based projects in Yorkshire and Lancashire over the last decade that have developed gardens producing plants with connections to textiles, heritage and wellbeing. The evidence base for engagement with green spaces and better wellbeing continues to grow, with concern about the environment increasing and ecotherapy seen as a benefit to mental health. Growing spaces, or green spaces of care, can be a haven from the busyness of everyday life even in the most urban areas. I have worked on projects developed in community allotment spaces, outdoor marketplaces, hospital gardens, brownfield sites, borrowed polytunnels and in one case, a raised bed in a car park. These projects have developed creative work inspired by research into the wellbeing benefits of working in, and with, nature.

Recent projects have addressed the association between plants and cloth and finding different ways to make connections between the two. Projects as part of 'Flourish', for community arts charity Hive, worked in urban locations around Bradford. Herb and flower beds were grown at community centres to be used as inspiration and materials for textile projects. Ideas for using a garden space, bed, windowsill or plant pot were shared and included:

- Growing and sourcing local plants for colouring and patterning fabrics using a variety of dyeing and printing techniques.
- Choosing plants with historic connections to health and resilience.
- Growing and harvesting plants to dry that can protect fibres and create scent. These included sweet woodruff, lady's bedstraw, lavender and marigolds. These are all fragrant and have traditionally been used in domestic settings.
- Processing plants for dyeing that use methods with the least impact on the environment.

Scrap fabric heart filled with lavender grown in the community garden. Sukoon-e-Dil group, Roshni Ghar Project, Keighley, West Yorkshire.

Creating patterned fabric with herbs

Bundling herbs and other plant material in fabric is a simple way to create colour and pattern on cloth. It is a way of producing a record of a place and can be combined with other processes, for example, collecting and drying herbs from a garden space to use with the textile.

Materials
- *A piece of scoured (washed to a high temperature to remove sizing or other finishes), recycled or peace silk, mordanted with alum or sprayed with vinegar to help receive and fix the colour. (Peace silk is produced using a method that does not kill the silkworm.)*
- *Herbs and flowers (fresh, dried or frozen). Violas and pansies produce bright colours using this method. You could also include red or brown onion skins.*
- *Thread or string. If you use thread this can be used to stitch with afterwards.*
- *A steamer, or colander, over a saucepan of boiling water.*

Method
1. Scatter or arrange the herbs and flowers across the piece of silk, then roll or fold the fabric to make a bundle.

2. Secure the bundle, wrapping tightly with thread or string, the tighter the better to ensure contact between the plant material and the fabric.

3. Steam the bundle for half an hour.

4. Let it cool before unwrapping, or leave the whole bundle intact for a few days to allow the plant material to remain in contact with the fabric.

Above *Small pieces of silk bundled with flower petals and herbs and tied with silk thread to create a pattern on the fabric.*

Opposite *Bundle-dyeing workshop with Cultureghem, a not-for-profit community organization in Brussels, Belgium, using food waste from the local marketplace (2019).*

At my own allotment and at community garden projects, we grew a small collection of herbs with multiple purposes, be they culinary, medicinal, or traditional textile plants. I was particularly interested in those that have historic connections to resilience, indicated by their description in traditional herbals. Plants often have multiple uses and I have found that there is an affinity between herbs and colour production. Reading old herbals, including Culpeper's (1653), throws up interesting uses for plants that I associate with colour production. Traditional dyes like madder (*Rubia tinctorum*), a plant that produces a strong red from its root, were also used for '… inward and outward bruises' and as something that 'cleanses the skin and takes freckles away'.[13] Woad, a traditional blue dye, 'Cools inflammations, quenches St Anthony's Fire and stays defluxions of blood to any part of the body.'[14] We grew plants including motherwort, garden sage, lavender, St John's wort, chamomile and heartsease, and created a palette of fabric coloured and scented with them. In summer I harvested and pressed specimens of the herbs and made a collection of contact prints by inking up the dried and pressed plants and running them through a printing press onto cotton calico woven in the local area. Threads dyed with the plants were used to stitch over these small compositions.

Above Sketchbook page including plant
sample, dyed colour swatches on wool and
silk and improvised recycled polystyrene
printing plate.

Opposite Stitched and printed sample using
dyer's chamomile and St John's wort (2019).
Wool, cotton, silk thread, hand stitch.

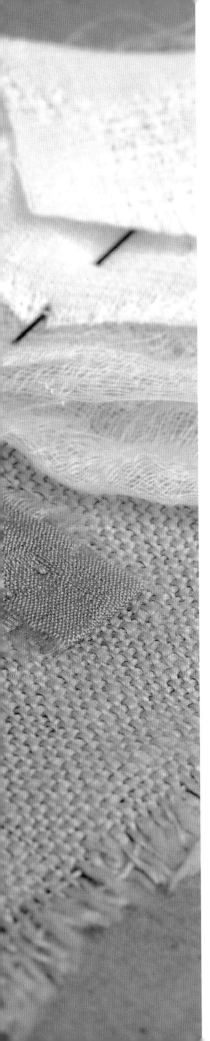

Colour and climate

In 2019 I travelled to Australia to teach with Fibre Arts Australia, visiting Toowoomba in Queensland and Adelaide, South Australia, to teach a Slow Colour and Stitch workshop that engaged with colours and marks found in the local environment. The emphasis was on found colour from local plants and is a workshop that I have also taught in different venues around the UK and in Europe. It was spring in Australia and I arrived from the damp, cool autumn in Northern England to dry heat and bright light. This light and the colours of the landscape were a revelation to me: during a flight from Brisbane to Adelaide I was struck by the tones seen below: ochre, dull greens, browns, yellows. For many years I had worked with local colour in projects where we grow dyes and other colour-producing plants and use what is available in the local environment. I had always found the variation in colour, depending on weather conditions, the time of year planted and harvested, one of the most interesting aspects of the craft. My time in Australia reinforced this thinking. The long period of drought experienced in South Australia, and particularly Queensland, meant that the colours echoed the landscape, producing muted shades. Plants yield less dye when under stress in these conditions, something that I had not experienced in other teaching settings. These colours were echoed in the dyes we produced, using plant material unfamiliar to me: windfall banksia and leopard tree pods, soursobs. They created muted shades in the dye baths we made.

Colour swatch samples from Toowoomba, Australia. Colours from soursobs, windfall banksia and leopard tree pods. Silk, linen, eucalyptus, recycled thread, hand stitch.

Bridget Harvey

Bridget Harvey Is a maker, curator and activist. She investigates process, materially exploring narrative patinas including use, emotional engagement and need. Her work occupies a fluid space between craft and design, making and remaking. She uses discarded objects as her primary medium, providing ground for (re)making and dialogue, collaboration and social engagement using 'active hope'.[15] She hand-works them into one-off or small-batch artefacts, drawing techniques from textiles, print and 3D disciplines, along with conservation methods, and inspired by narratives of use and disuse to create tactile and desirable objects. Her artefacts are hybrids of making, autobiography and process, their forms recrafted and recast as messengers to communicate discourses of repair-making, sustainability and sharing. She says 'Through layers of making, thinking and acting, they are agency made material.' Bridget has recently been maker in residence at the V&A in London, where her work focused on repaired objects in the collection and repair practices in the museum.

She writes about resilience:

Resilience
Is deterministic
Listens
Is live actions
Is contagious
Is social capital
Exists in the face of adversity
Is (sometimes) a group decision
Is asserting personal choice
Is choosing not to endure but to improve
Is a combination of crisis planning and aiming for highest hopes
Can facilitate further resilience in others or create resilient communities.

That day I marched with the self-formed, self-proclaimed menders bloc – me and David, friends from TRAID and the Restart Project [textile recycling social enterprises]. We were there as our own critical mass, contributing to the greater one, and for our own personal politics.

Right and opposite *Bridget Harvey (UK),* Mend More Jumper *(2015). Acrylic jumper, hand-dyed cotton, cotton threads. Shown on the November 2015 Climate March in London.*

Staunchly environmentalist, all actively activist, all specifically engaged with Repair-Making, carrying out our duty to care for people and planet by suggesting repair as part of that. *MEND MORE Jumper* asks us to use repair skills for practicality, resilience and resistance, and to protect the planet. The words on it are textual and material. It shows my hand skills but is not repaired; it was not broken or damaged when I bought it. Materially then, it is messy; it contradicts itself. As placard it is more visible than itself as clothing. It is overt propaganda, journeying between the terrain of the lived and of potentials, functioning as both messy and clear, personal and political, text and textile.

Repair Dialogues

My work draws on plain sewing techniques, patching and stitching using found materials and everyday materials, using found dyes and objects. I mark time through repetitive stitching. Repairing textiles reminds me of the materiality and temporality of the object. Stitching to repair something adds a layer of narrative to the object, my personal relationship to it changing from a passive to an active one.

At the end of 2015 areas of West Yorkshire, where I live, experienced severe flooding. In January 2016 I retrieved a saturated and frozen rough grey woollen blanket, previously used as packing for a printing press, from a skip full of damaged materials at an artists' studio badly affected by the flood. I wanted to repair the blanket as a gesture and returned it, thawed, washed, then patched and reinforced with stitching in the areas weakened by water and other damage, to my colleagues there. Peter Dormer describes a 'dialogue' that occurs between maker and the object being made[16] (or repaired) with practical skill as the medium through which this occurs. My idea for *Repair Dialogues* developed from this blanket repair, and I have subsequently been given other woollen items to mend in a similar way, including a lap blanket belonging to my late grandfather and full of moth holes. I liked the idea of remediation where the repair work can improve the state of the original as this to me seems more practical. I was also interested in exploring practical applications and parallel meanings themed around mending and repair, and also in conversations around the subject, whether they are using repair in an emotional, environmental or political sense.

Above, below and
opposite *Work from Repair Dialogues (2016– ongoing), including woollen blankets and place mats. Wool, wool patches, woollen thread, hand stitch.*

Reinforcing to renew

Reinforcing a textile as a variety of repair (as demonstrated in *Repair Dialogues*) can be done in two different ways: by stitching over the weakened area to strengthen the material, or by patching (in front or behind) the weakened area to add a new layer and then adding stitches.

Materials

- *Cloth to be reinforced.*
- *Darning mushroom, egg or other object (a lightbulb or a potato would work well) to support the back of the cloth as you work.*
- *Thread that matches (or contrasts with) the colour of your garment or object that requires reinforcing.*
- *Fabric of a similar weight and type to the surface requiring repair.*

The examples shown here and overleaf are made and mended using wool. Wool (particularly the blanket fabric shown here) is less inclined to fray. The technique is transferrable when using other fabrics. If you are using cotton or linen you may want to turn the edges when patching one fabric on top of another before adding additional stitching.

***Below** Traditional repair tools and darning eggs and mushrooms (collection of the author).*

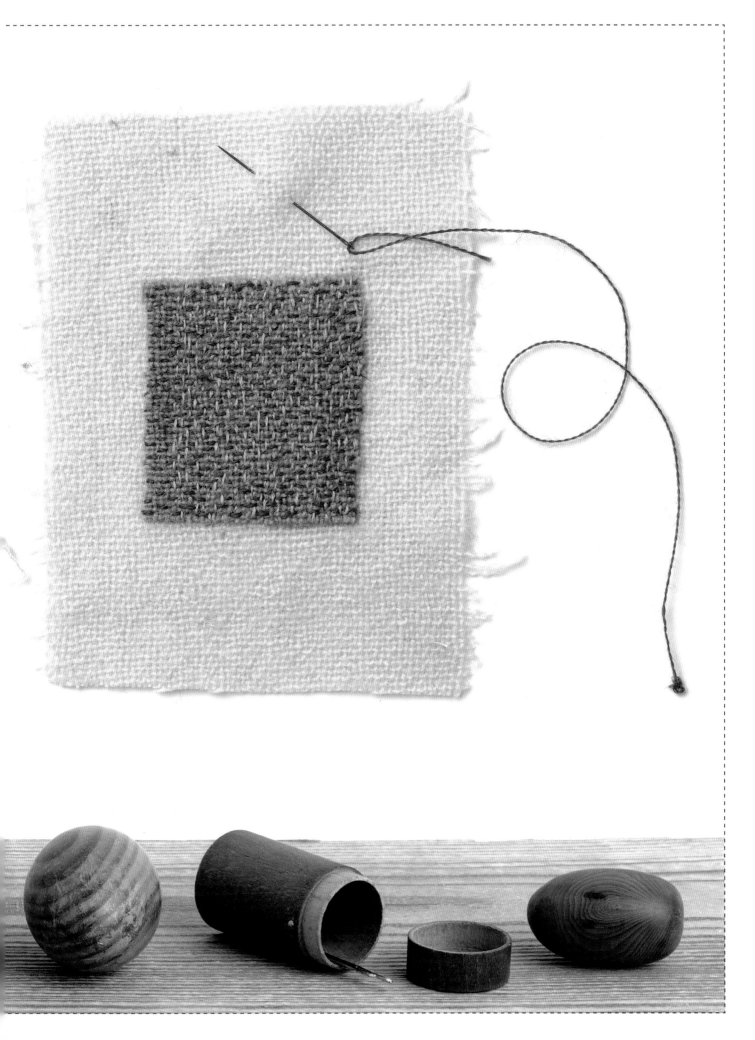

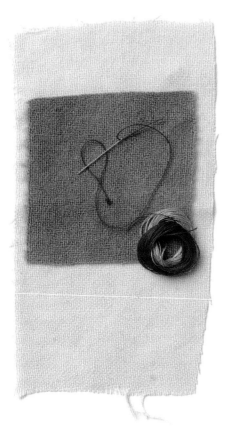

Method

1. If working directly onto the fabric to be reinforced then mark a square, diamond or circle around the weakened area or hole with a friction pen or tailor's chalk. Make sure that this covers a large enough area.

2. Fill the area marked with small running stitches (see diagram opposite). Make sure that you stitch a dense area, making your rows close together.

3. Turn your fabric and begin to stitch at 90 degrees to your other stitches to create a closely worked network of stitches.

4. If working using additional fabric to first patch the weakened area or hole, then cut to larger than this area and stitch as described above.

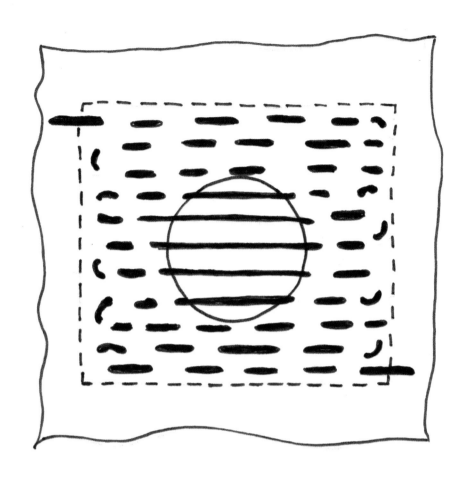

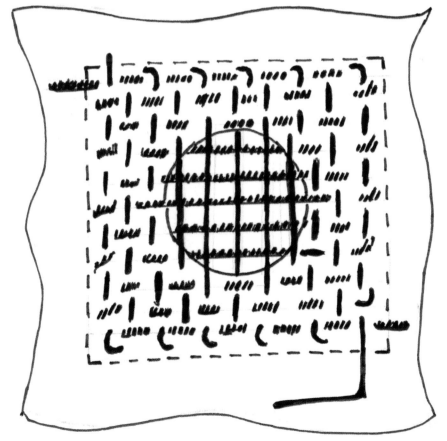

Raisa Kabir

Raisa Kabir is a multi-disciplinary artist, weaver and writer who uses contemporary textiles, sound and photography to interrogate and question concepts around the politics of dress in connection to gender, race and sexuality. Trained as a weaver at Chelsea College of Art, she utilizes the embedded histories of cloth to comment on the compacted social histories that are encapsulated within material culture.

Textiles and dress tell much about the politics and culture of a society, reflecting on gender, class, race and sexuality. Cloth because of its link to the body, its hinting at hidden labour and the violences unspoken, means that the potential emotion that cloth carries can be used as an incredibly powerful tool with which to materialize and evoke historical and present human narratives. She told me:

> As a queer, diasporic South Asian artist, my practice centres the encapsulated violent histories embedded within cloth and textiles through embodying globalized racialized labours as a critique of empire and neo-colonialism. Rooted in diaspora thought and research, my work aims to connect the realities and repercussions of Bangladeshi and wider South Asian diaspora living in Britain. Trained in textiles as a weaver, my work investigates the material relationship of cotton, performed labour and migrational threads that connect Lancashire's now desolate factories and the histories of hand loom textile production in Bangladesh and India. From the East India Company exporting the finest cotton muslin woven in Bengal to the establishment of a Bangladeshi diaspora in 1970s Oldham and Burnley, working in industrial cotton spinning factories. Mapping and warping borders, partition and conflict; my work utilizes textile installations, using my body and labour in weaving and performance contexts, to highlight the endurance of survival as a disabled, queer brown body living in (a post-Brexit) Britain. My performances use the ability of weaving, as a theoretical strategy, to be used as a disruptive performative practice that builds on theories of embodied knowing, textiles as gendered archives, enacted through dance and performance.

Raisa Kabir (UK), Build me a loom off of your back and your stomach *(2018). Images from performance.*

Build me a loom off of your back and your stomach (2018)

Build me a loom off of your back and your stomach is a performance of durational dance, distance and diaspora. The artist Raisa Kabir weaves and dances, carrying the lengths of cloth-making labour throughout the gallery space. A visualization of dislocated geographies, the weight of ongoing trauma, and their ghosts.

   Description from the University of Manchester events website, events.manchester.ac.uk

Alice Kettle

Alice Kettle is a textile/fibre artist, writer and lecturer based in the UK. She is Professor of Textile Arts at Manchester School of Art, Manchester Metropolitan University, Visiting Professor at the University of Winchester and President of the Embroiderers' Guild. Her vast textile panels narrate contemporary events through rich and intricate stitchwork.

Kettle's works often use embroidery to engage in participatory collaborative projects, such as her recent work *Thread Bearing Witness*, shown at the Whitworth Gallery, Manchester 2018–19, and as part of the first British Textile Biennial at Gawthorpe Hall. Three giant textiles: *Sea* (2017), *Ground* (2018) and *Sky* (2018), were

made to examine refugee issues and migration. Kettle writes in the accompanying catalogue that 'at the core of the project has been a willingness to be guided by refugees', describing the 'resilience and courage' of those directly affected. *Ground* and *Sky* are joint projects. Individuals from refugee camps abroad and migrant communities new to the UK contributed drawings of people, homes, birds, flowers. These were then scanned by Kettle and embroidered onto printed backgrounds. 'All the images are mixed up together and coexisting in a unified world.'[17] In *Sea*, the harrowing story of sea crossings and their often tragic endings, we see from above people in a mass of blue. Viewing the work for a second time in the huge 15th-century Great Barn at Gawthorpe Hall on a quiet afternoon I had the place to myself. The overwhelming sadness of the stories included in the work was palpable, alongside a feeling of hope, particularly when viewing *Sky*, which has a feeling of lightness in expression of trauma and the power of creativity when dealing with it.

Collaborative work led by Alice Kettle (UK), Sky *(2018). One of three works:* Ground, Sea *and* Sky. *First exhibited at the Whitworth Gallery, Manchester. Cotton, rayon and metallic thread on printed canvas. 3 × 8m (10 × 26ft). A list of contributing artists can be found on page 125.*

Collaborative works led by
Alice Kettle (UK).

Above Ground (2018).
Cotton, rayon, metallic
thread and life jacket
material on printed
canvas. 3 × 8m
(9¾ × 26¼ft).

Right Sea (2017). Cotton,
rayon and metallic thread
on printed canvas.
3 × 8m (9¾ × 26¼ft).

Both pieces first exhibited
at the Whitworth Gallery,
Manchester. A list of
contributing artists can be
found on page 125.

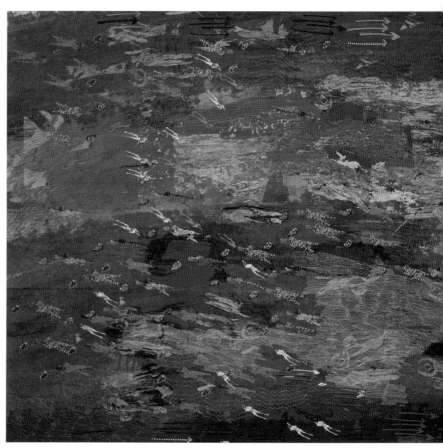

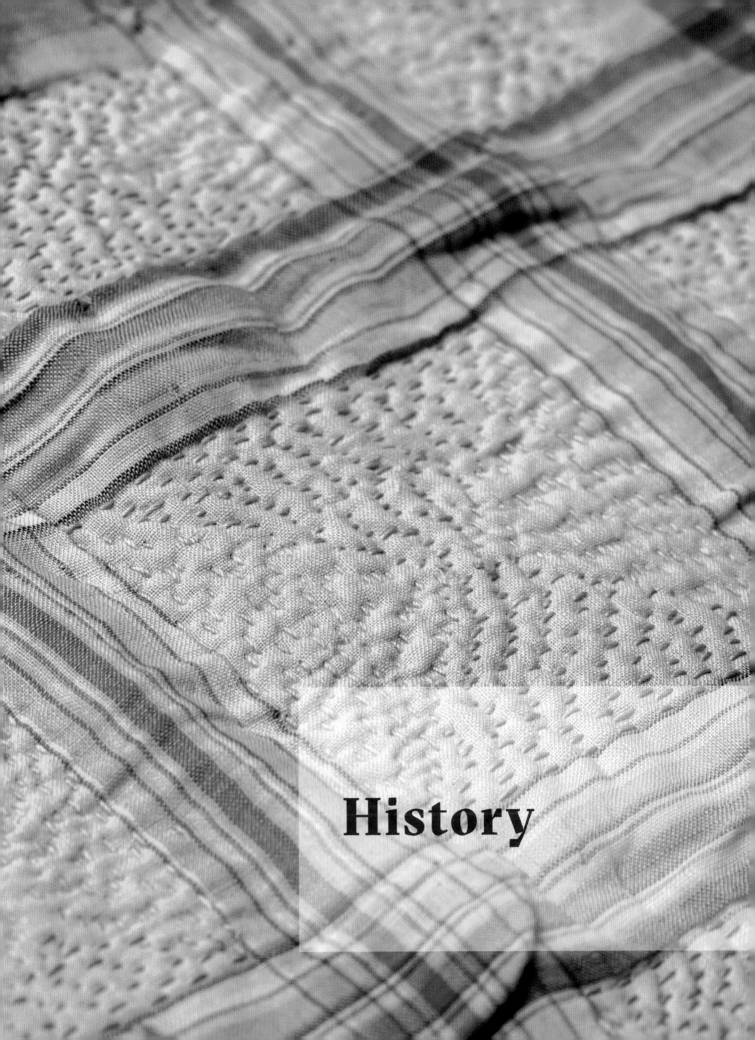

History

Textiles have an ability to tell stories, through their materials, through their use. 'The making of textiles is deeply rooted within our history and sense of identity; a quilt can contain many memories and act as a protective layer both mentally and physically.'[18] My projects have looked for local stories, often engaging with the textile heritage on my doorstep, and sometimes with the privilege of working in or exhibiting in buildings connected to textile production. Stories from industry are countered by and sometimes coincide with stories from the personal and domestic. When teaching I often ask participants to talk about an early textile memory. A diverse variety have been shared over the years: the slippery, cold feeling of getting into a bed made up with nylon sheets (and the particular pink shade they often were); more bed sheets, this time pastel-striped brushed cotton; the rough texture of an armchair upholstered in brocade fabric, the softness of a mother's dress hem, the satin edge of a cot blanket and how it felt between finger, thumb and mouth; long socks embroidered with traditional Serbian designs for a dancing competition, an animal-print headscarf. Anthropologist Daniel Miller, writing in *Stuff*, talks of how clothing has a particular affinity with memory and emotion. 'A study of clothing should not be cold; it has to invoke the tactile, emotional, intimate world of feelings.'[19] Other textile reminiscing sessions delivered as part of community projects have focused on clothing and have used a quote from Louise Bourgeois, 'Clothing is an exercise of memory. It makes me explore the past: how did I feel when I wore that … like little signposts in the search for the past.'[20]

Conversations around clothes at community sessions used prompts including, 'Show and tell us the oldest thing in your wardrobe that you still regularly wear', or 'Bring a garment from your wardrobe that has had many lives to talk about'. These have brought stories of ordinary garments to vivid life.

Frieda's Handkerchief, shown here, is a 'tag blanket' made for my youngest daughter from a handkerchief that belonged to her late great-grandmother and ribbons from her workbasket. It was designed as an object for sensory play (and much loved, evidenced by how it now needs repairing).

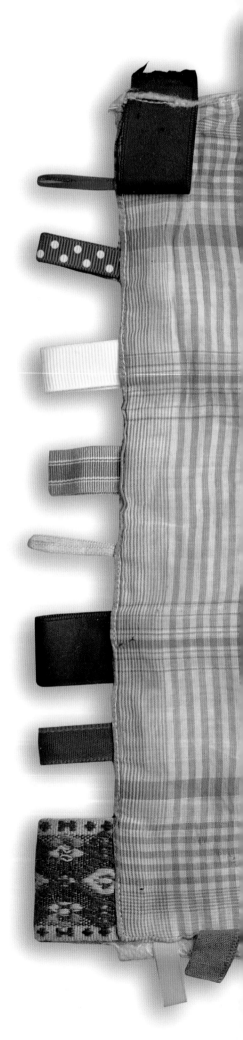

Frieda's Handkerchief *(2009). Recycled cotton handkerchief and ribbons, wool hand stitch. 30 × 30cm (12 × 12in).*

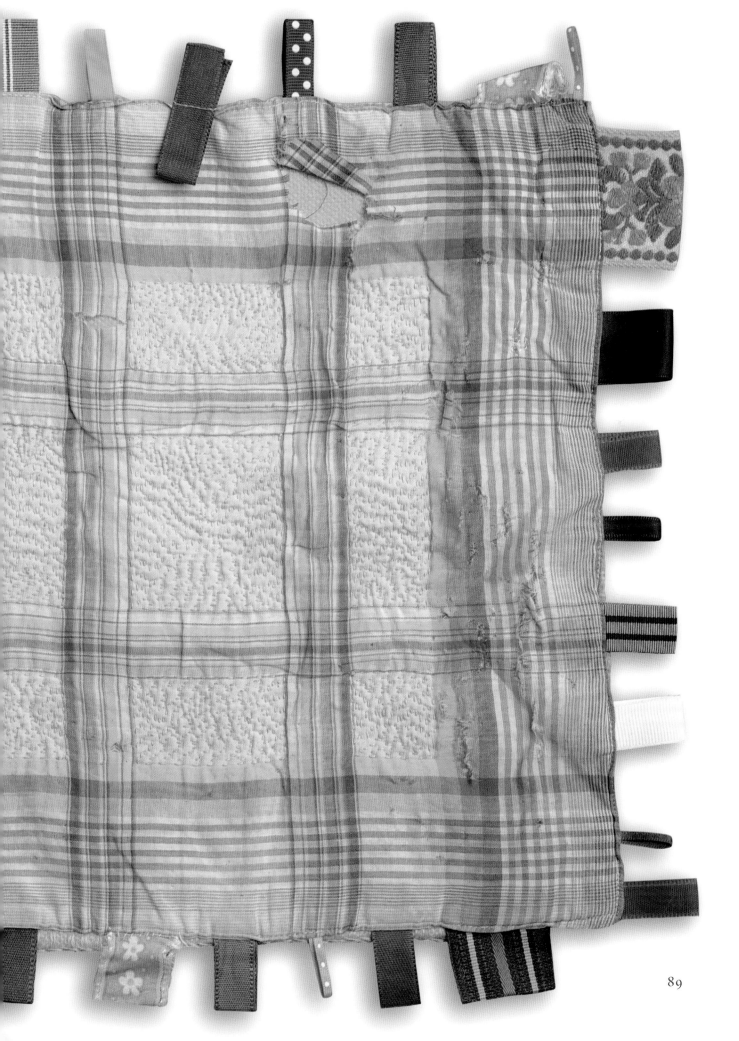

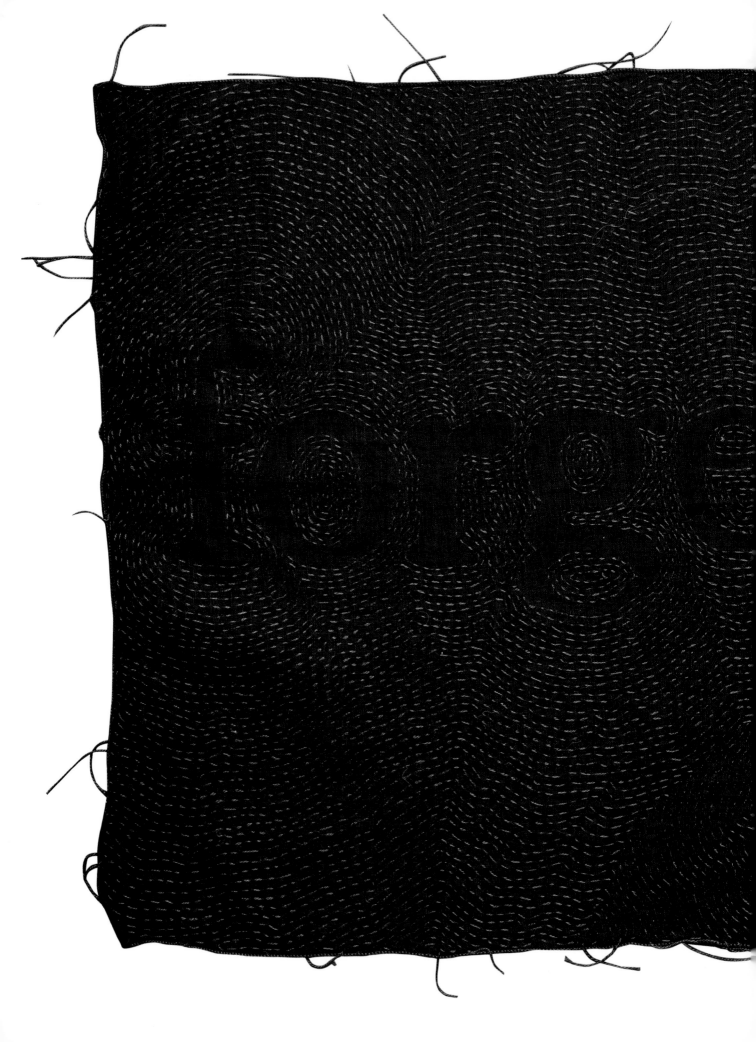

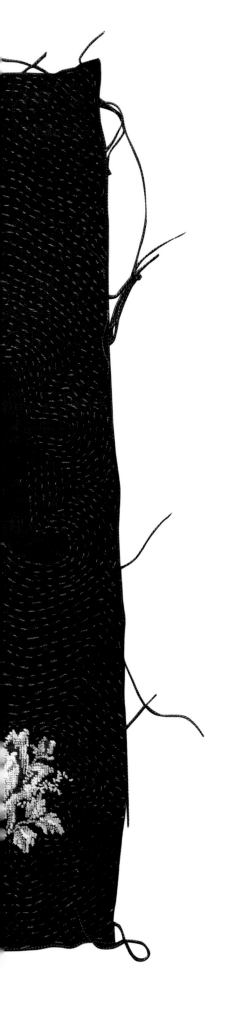

Ruth Singer

Ruth Singer is an artist–maker based in the UK. Prior to setting up her own studio practice she worked in museums including the V&A. She now combines her creative practice with project development and specializes in creating arts projects with partners including heritage and community organizations, universities and galleries. She creates exhibitions, installations and commissions, often using old cloth and hand stitch with subtle and intriguing hidden stories. She writes:

> My work explores human experience expressed through thoughtful and emotionally engaged textile making. My subtle and delicate work references loss, memory, fragility and damage in both the cloth itself and in our personal lives, and the places in which we gather memories. My background as a textile historian and museum curator is woven throughout my work; I create pieces with a sense of history and a look of antiques but with a powerful contemporary story.

Forget

This work began with my looking at museum collections of 'Forget Me Not' embroideries and memorial samplers. On reflection, I consider that there are some things that are better to forget than to remember, some things must be let go. I am also referring to that fact that we can't keep hold of memories, we forget things, however hard we try to keep them. Things fade and change, and our memories can't be trusted.

For a number of years, I have used textile-making to express difficult emotional experiences, not as a way of keeping my hands busy, but more for the positive act of creating something good out of unhappiness. When I am working in this way, each tiny hand stitch in a time-consuming piece is a conscious act of letting go of the bad memories, the unhappy stories and the things that weigh us down. By the time the pieces are ready to exhibit, the memories are much less painful for me and the moment of anguish has passed. The stories remain embedded in the cloth, resonating with so many others who feel their own experience reflected back through the delicacy of stitch, and power of simple statements of loss, grief, anger and disappointment. Through making my emotions and experiences into works of textile art, I hope to support others in finding their own emotional repair.

Ruth Singer (UK), Forget *(2017–18). Vintage handkerchief with rose embroidery as found, artist's hand embroidery in silk thread.*

Making for memory

The following exercise uses scrap fabrics and a traditional English paper piecing pattern, sometimes known as Grandmother's Flower Garden. Look at your fabric collection. You may have a collection of materials from previous dressmaking or creative textile projects; old pieces of clothing past wearing can also be unpicked to make a new fabric. Some of these may hold a particular memory for you.

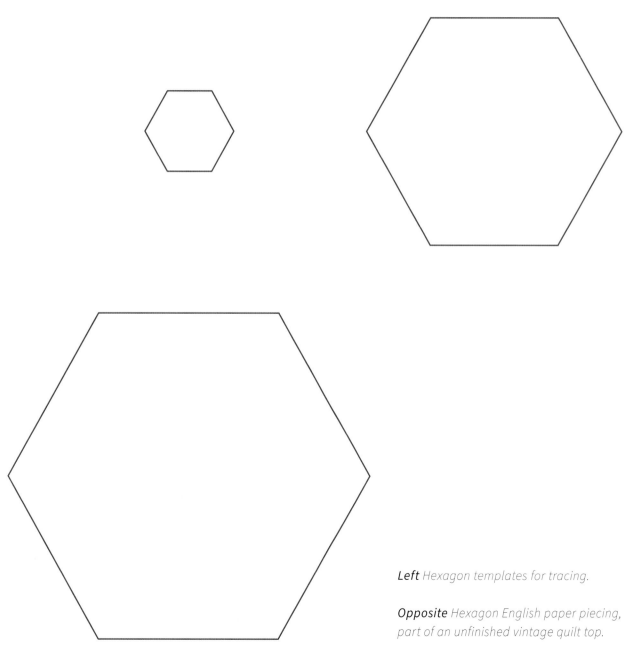

Left Hexagon templates for tracing.

Opposite Hexagon English paper piecing, part of an unfinished vintage quilt top.

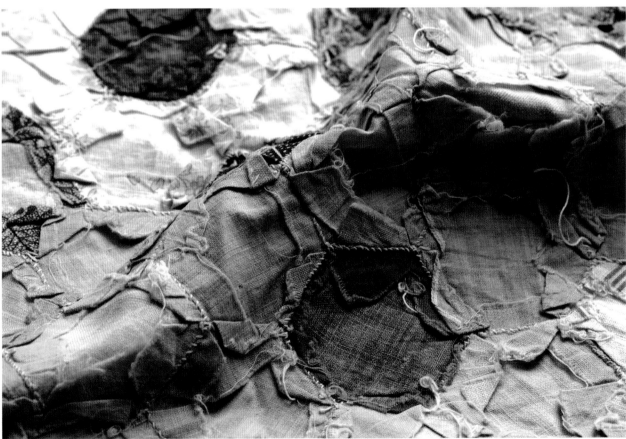

When choosing the scraps, I went through my collection of fabrics sourced from family textiles, scraps from dressmaking projects of my mother and grandmother, baby clothes worn by my daughters, passed down through four sisters and now saved for patching and quilt projects. They included tiny prints from a needlecord dress, embroidery from a pyjama top and striped seersucker from a homemade skirt.

Method

1. Choose seven fabrics. This does not have to make a functional textile, so using different weights of material (silks next to wools, synthetic linings next to towelling, for example) does not really matter. The idea is to find some resonance in the fabrics you choose. Do they remind you of a person, an event, a place? Does the feel of them evoke a memory, the softness, roughness, slipperiness of the surface?

2. Using a hexagonal template (a selection of sizes are available on page 92 for tracing, or you could purchase a set of plastic or metal templates). Cut seven pieces from scrap paper (I use recycled envelopes and find the different patterns inside them very pleasing).

3. Cut a piece of fabric larger than the template by 6mm (¼in) all the way around – this gives you a seam allowance of 6mm (¼in)

4. Using tacking stitches, and paying particular attention to the corners, attach the fabric around the paper template. Repeat for the remaining six hexagons.

5. When all seven have been tacked you can begin to sew them together. A neutral-coloured thread will minimize when sewing different coloured or patterned fabrics together, although in this sample I have used red thread, just visible when the fabric is turned over. In many traditional textiles, red is used on vulnerable edges of the cloth – seams, edges.

6. Consider the sample now, with the internal edges connected and reinforced. The joined parts create a whole, and together the personal fabrics create a new site for memories.

Scrap fabrics from baby clothes remade using the English paper piecing technique.

Resistance

On Westgate, central Bradford, in the early 2000s I spotted a blue plaque on the wall by the pound shop door next to the bus stop where I was standing.

The text read 'From this Textile Hall on September 9th 1917 3,000 women of the Bradford Women's Humanity League took part in an anti-war demonstration and march across the city'. Looking more closely at the front of the building I could see the words 'Textile Hall' in leaded lights, just visible behind the security grille mechanism. At the time I was intrigued by this and stored the knowledge away to possibly revisit at a later date. Many years later, when I was approached about the possibility of a solo exhibition in Bradford Cathedral, the dates coincided with the centenary of the march. I decided to research the subject in more detail, and it became a body of work called *Resist*. The relevance of the march was brought into contemporary context by other marches, largely attended by women (including myself) around the world in January 2017, which coincided with the inauguration of Donald Trump as US president.

I was able to spend a bit of time in the Bradford Local Studies Library looking at newspaper articles from the time and also at research into women's opposition to the First World War. I was struck

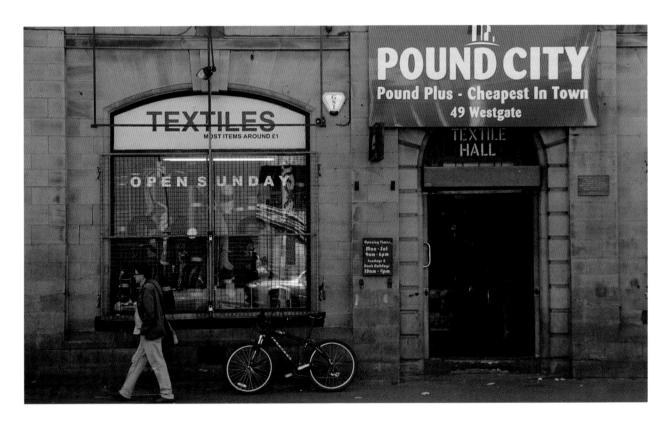

by the fact that the women involved in Bradford Women's Humanity League were ordinary women, often textile workers, expressing their humanitarian concern. They had initially supported other women experiencing unemployment, who were in hardship because of the war, with practical help. But with the Military Service Act in 1916 and the beginning of conscription, they began to campaign for a negotiated peace.

Bradford Women's Humanity League became very active, holding public meetings at the Textile Hall, speaking on street corners, canvassing door to door, travelling to other areas to support other peace campaigns, and it became involved in the Women's Peace Crusade. This grassroots socialist movement was active in the UK between 1916 and 1918 and aimed to spread a 'people's peace'. Large demonstrations took place across the UK in 1917. The march in Bradford on 9 September set out from Westgate and ended at Carlton Street, now Bradford School of Art, where I studied for my Masters degree.

Above *Goitside, Bradford, West Yorkshire. Former textile district, now partially derelict.*

Opposite *Former Textile Hall, Westgate, Bradford, West Yorkshire. Meeting place of the Bradford Women's Humanity League and starting point of their 1917 peace march.*

3,000 women marched in procession with banners flying and bands playing … The Bradford women are splendid. They attribute their success on Sunday chiefly to their open-air meetings at street corners. They have held three of these every week since June. They have made their own banners and have sold hundreds of badges … may their example be copied by women all over the country.[21]

97

I had made other work about areas of Bradford and Northern former textile towns, intrigued by the rhythms and patterns of work and community generated by successful industry and full employment. These post-industrial rhythms of place today are very different. The dominant rhythms of capitalist production and of the everyday lives of the communities involved in this production have changed forever. In all of these pieces of work I developed my ideas by walking the same route around the site and repeating it over a period of time, photographing, observing detail, collecting materials.

I began a weekly walk from the Textile Hall on Westgate to Carlton Street, taking various routes, in early 2017. The built environment of the city had changed in many ways in the last century but the area I walked in had remained largely unaltered, consisting of 19th-century wool warehousing, former textile mills and other industrial buildings, many now empty, some derelict. The street pattern has changed very little since the early 20th century. There are also blank spaces left by mill fires or demolition in these gaps, often turned into cheap gravel car parks. Plant life has re-established itself and small pieces of scrap metal are easily found, as well as other discarded things, including textile scraps. I focused my work on this area, in the

Above Tumbling Hill
Street *(2017), detail. Found
and recycled fabric, found
dyes, hand stitch.
13 × 13cm (5 × 5in).*

Opposite *Found plant
material collected on
my walking route for
making dyes.*

absence of knowledge about the exact route of the original march,
but also because of the nature of textile production in the area.
Perhaps the women who marched worked there too?

Walking my route in June and July I collected plant material,
taking the same route each time and recording my journey. Up
Tumbling Hill Street I found rosebay willowherb and buddleia
sprouting through walls, wild raspberry, self-seeded rowan and
sycamore and weld, a traditional dye plant that makes a bright
yellow colour. I gathered then soaked and processed the plants to
use as dyes for fabrics and threads. I also used whole plants clamped
to my fabric with rusted scaffolders' plates found on the route to
create contact prints on my fabrics. Other collected scraps of metal
were used to make an iron modifier for my dyes. Iron darkens or
'saddens' plant dyes, eventually making them black. In this work it
was a nod to a great specialism of the Bradford Trade in the
19th century, when millions of yards of black-dyed worsted cloth
were exported from the city around the world.

I assembled quick studies using materials from the walks, not
to illustrate my journey in the traditional sense, but as a kind of
mapping exercise for myself. The larger pieces of work were more
specific to the areas walked: Providence Street, Goitside, Chain
Street. In my home studio I spent a long time sewing the pieces
together with continuous running stitches, using old silk thread
produced by Listers, a Bradford company based at what was then
the largest silk mill in the world. The layers of fabric meant that
there was a certain amount of resistance to the needle so this was
not the easiest process.

Hand-stitching afforded me thinking time, so as I worked I was
considering the labour of the women involved in the march. Not only
their work in munitions factories and in weaving cloth for military
uniforms, but also the additional things Bradford women did during
the First World War, being given additional wool by the spinning mills
to knit for the soldiers, all this alongside domestic work and, for those
women campaigners, spending long hours protesting, resisting.

The writer Rebecca Solnit says of walking, 'Past and present
are brought together when you walk … and each walk moves
through space like a thread through fabric, sewing it together into
a continuous experience.'[22] In this piece of work I tried to make a
connection between the women who marched through my city in
September 1917 through an investigation into the landscape and
geography of the city as it is today.

Opposite Resist:
Providence Street (*2017*);
detail shown above.
Found and recycled fabric,
found dyes, hand stitch.
40 × 50cm (15¾ × 19¾in).

Recovery: Louisa Pesel and the Bradford Khaki Handicrafts Club

Embroiderer Louisa Pesel (1870–1947) was born in Bradford, and after her education at a local girls' grammar school went on to study art and design in London. She worked as the Director of the Royal Hellenic School of Needlework and Laces in Athens, before returning to England and becoming involved in needlework education and lecturing, and setting up a branch of what would later become the Embroiderers' Guild. She wrote several embroidery books published by Batsford. During the First World War she worked with Belgian refugees in Bradford and instigated a project – The Bradford Khaki Handicrafts Club – to teach textile skills to soldiers of the Abram Peel Military Hospital, all of whom were suffering from neurasthenia or shell shock. Between 1917 and 1919, over 400 men took part in activities at the club, learning embroidery skills, weaving and netting. Therapeutic textile activity for returning soldiers had been adopted as a strategy by British, Australian and New Zealand hospitals during the war. In Bradford their work was made to be sold and they were paid for it. A newspaper article described the activities of the project:

> The value of handicrafts in the treatment of shell shock, albeit generally admitted, is in no danger of being overrated … A band of public-spirited ladies in Bradford, keen craftswomen, realized how unsatisfactory was this state of affairs. They decided to attempt an improvement, and, guided only by natural sympathy and unbounded faith in the virtue of handicrafts, they yet tackled the business more scientifically than the hospital had done.

Left Bradford Khaki Handicrafts Club altar cloth (on wall), exhibited as part of 'Unbound: Visionary Women Collecting Textiles' (2020) at Two Temple Place, London.

The article also focuses on the therapeutic benefits of the work, and the language used is very much of its time …

> They came to the club nervous wrecks, some hardly able to walk; they were put to work, netting, or weaving, or stitching and the charm fell upon them. The brightness of the room, the atmosphere of busy contentment cheered them; the ordered methodical work soothed them; they became interested in the pattern growing daily under their hands, anxious to keep it perfect. The cure has begun.[23]

It goes on to observe that some of the patients went on to be discharged from hospital 'out again into the turmoil and complexity of the twentieth century'.

An altar superfrontal designed by Pesel and inspired by Greek island patterns (her specialism) and worked in cross stitch, was used for the soldiers' services at the Abram Peel Hospital and is now displayed at Bradford Cathedral. It was made in late 1918, the Khaki Handicrafts Club activities coming to a close the following May, Pesel writing: 'The work of the Handicrafts Club is completed. We have had 450 men on our register and our attendances for the thirteen months amount to 10,000, so there is no doubt about it having been needed.'[24]

Above Bradford soldiers being instructed in stitching by Louisa Pesel, 1917 (Louisa Pesel scrapbook image). Reproduced with the permission of Special Collections, Leeds University Library.

103

Willemien de Villiers

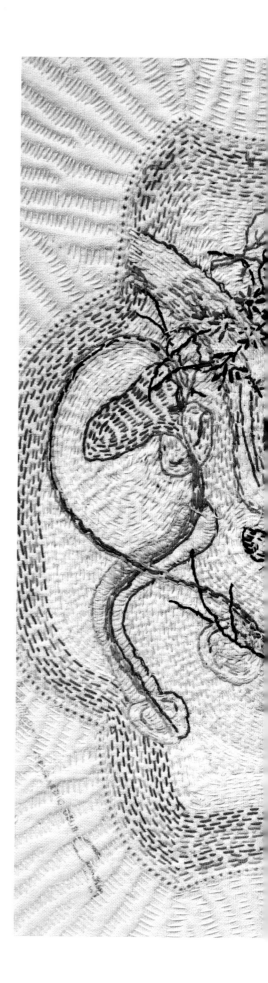

Willemien de Villiers is a South African artist and writer based in Muizenberg, Cape Town. With her stitched textile works she hopes to transcend, and subvert, the traditional idea of embroidery as women's work. Her work explores, in an intimate and personal way, themes of patriarchy, toxic masculinity as a contributing factor in domestic violence, as well as gender identity. She told me that 'I continue to study and celebrate the interconnection of all living things, especially in evidence when comparing the morphology of flowering plants with the reproductive cycles and organs of mammals.' Her work is a dialogue between real and imagined microscopic biological phenomena, reconstructing the common cellular history of all living things through atomized patterning. The process of decay and disintegration, and the inevitable new growth and integration that follows, inform this major theme in her work, especially with regard to memory; personal, political and social. For her stitched works, she uses vintage domestic textiles, like doilies, tray cloths, tablecloths, that show a lot of wear and tear, with a sense of previous lives, or narratives, to work with.

In a letter she writes, 'The word for "resilience", in my mother tongue, Afrikaans, has its root in the flexible quality of birds' feathers; their ability to bounce back when bent. *Veerkrag*. I celebrate this quality of female endurance and resilience in my work. I use old (preferably much used and stained) embroidered domestic linen – like tray cloths, napkins, tablecloths – as my base cloth, onto which I stitch my various stories using mostly running, or mending, stitch. I love how the rows of small stitches strengthen the sometimes fragile and damaged fabric.'

Willemien de Villiers (South Africa), Female Notions 2 *(2019). Hand stitch with cotton embroidery thread on found domestic linen tray cloth using mainly mending stitch, starched and ironed. 48 × 36cm (19 × 14¼in).*

**Conclusion:
a resilient
textile**

Stitch journal revisited: a personal approach

I wrote about my stitch journal, an example of daily practice, in my last book. I am now in the eighth year of an (almost) daily stitching exercise. The rules are simple for me: I choose a thread and a place to begin on the linen fabric I work on, and then stitch, sometimes for just a few minutes. My stitching is not chronological, I move around my fabric, a piece of recycled linen cloth, as the mood takes me. Sometimes I spend five minutes stitching, at other times hours. My stitches are mostly variations of running stitch.

Over time I have changed some of the ways that I work on my piece of cloth. For example, I now occasionally appliqué other fabrics to the main fabric. Sometimes these are things that speak to me of a particular moment or were found or given to me. A recent section includes the fabric from a tea bag that I saved after a particularly inspiring conversation. Other scraps of dyed cloth come from workshops, a vivid yellow from midsummer work in northern Denmark and dull greens and browns dyed in Queensland, Australia during an intense period of drought. The colours remind me of the locations, the people I met and worked with, the conversations had. I tend to leave unfinished threads as I stitch, but recently have begun to couch these threads in circles when I find that I have resolved some aspect of my thinking. They act as markers over time, a way of telling my own story through cloth, and all the ups and downs of life, a personal journal of resilience.

Stitch Journal *(2013–ongoing), detail.*
Recycled linen, naturally dyed silk threads.

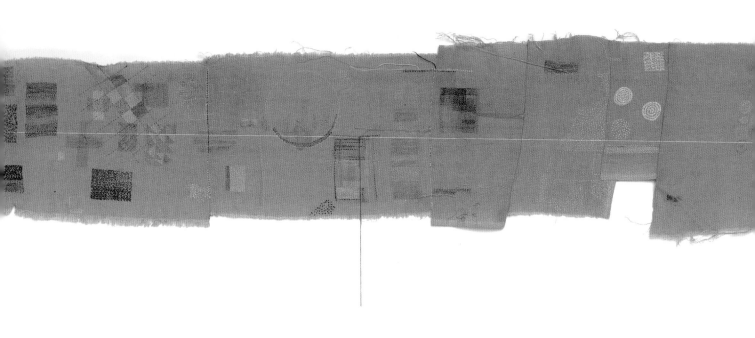

Writing about it in 2013 I described it has having 'No rules, no projected outcome. A record of days, but not a daily record.' I also wrote about it in *Slow Stitch: Mindful and Contemplative Textile Art* as part of an exploration of textile as a daily practice. Over the years I've continued to stitch, sometimes adding new sections of cloth, sometimes overstitching previously worked areas. My favoured threads are still the ones I dye myself, another way of making a personal place-based connection to the cloth. The cloth as a whole piece is now over 3m (almost 10ft) long, no longer the portable project it was when I began. On days when I've been evaluating projects, writing funding bids, sitting in meetings and all the other administrative tasks that go into working on arts projects, I find the simple act of choosing thread and beginning to stitch very restorative. I have since used the journal as a teaching tool, having interesting conversations with students about the idea of daily recording, and of using a textile process as a method of being 'in the

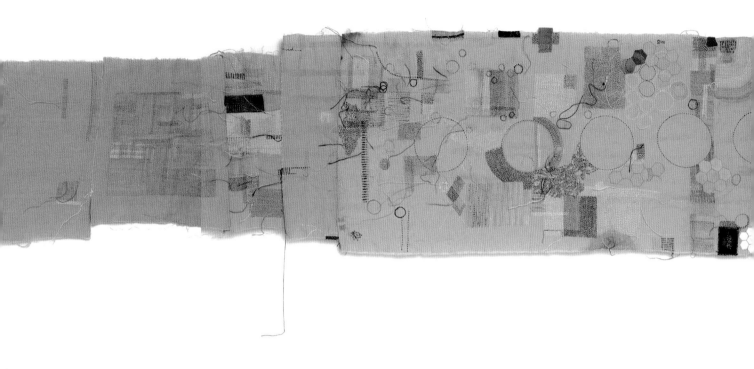

Stitch Journal (2013–ongoing). Recycled linen, naturally dyed silk threads, mercerized cotton. 470cm (185in) × various widths.

moment'. As it has developed, I have found my stitching changes depending on the type of work I am engaged with at that time. When in a writing phase, for research or projects, it helps to clear my head – the messiness of words and structures needing some organizing through a simple grid or block of running stitch. There is also a physical need to hold onto the material as I stitch, a tangible object when so much time is spent looking at a screen. The poet Nick Laird describing his writing days talks of 'scraping pattern out of that chaos of daily circumstance and finding the right details to speak for the whole.'[25] He describes a kind of flow state that emerges and of being completely lost in the work. The repetitious nature of this stitching project has been a hugely useful tool to me, in processing ideas, and in finding my own pattern through multiple projects and deadlines. For me it has developed into personal method of using a textile as a place of care. My engagement with the cloth offers me a calm space, a way of thinking through making.

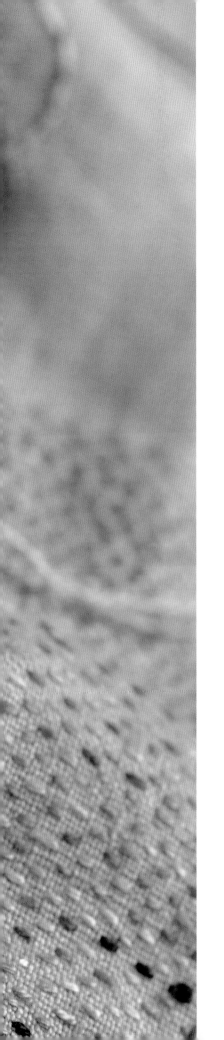

Ideas for a daily textile practice

- Stitching a shape a day. I often suggest to students that a shape to work within offers a useful structure for stitching every day. The confines of a small area are an easy way to begin, rather than looking at a large expanse of cloth and feeling daunted by it.
- Intuitive stitching or 'taking a line for a walk'. Begin to stitch, see where it takes you. I have used this method with fly stitch, a stitch which I feel has movement.
- Negative space embroidery. Stitching around a shape; I sometimes use seed stitch for this to fill larger areas.
- Stitching a word a day.
- Using other fabric and thread to create a picture of your day or a moment from it.
- Adding found or special fabric. Think about how you might do this. I like to add fragments rather than large pieces of cloth.
- Looking for found marks, colours, stains, rubs – from plant material, dyes you might be working with, your coffee cup.
- Different stitches for different moods – e.g. a block of running stitch is a bit like automatic writing. It can allow your mind to roam.

Opposite and above Stitch Journal *(2013–ongoing), details. Recycled linen, naturally dyed silk threads.*

Lull

While working as Artist in Residence at Bradford School of Art in 2015 I continued my work around themes connected to the textile-dyeing heritage of the region. I explored the philosopher Hannah Arendt's idea of 'restorative praxis'[26] using found objects and textile dyes extracted from the new plant growth that emerges around former industrial textile sites in Bradford and Pennine Lancashire. That summer I was also travelling to a residency at Gawthorpe Textiles Collection near Burnley, Lancashire, and spent some time walking and collecting at old mill sites in the area. Large crops of weld were common, and I discovered dyer's greenweed, a rarer sight, growing alongside the Rochdale canal. I dyed silk threads with these and other collected plant material and stitched a block of running stitch up the centre of a bolt of old cotton and linen. Arendt wrote of loss as something that is always countermanded by action, her idea of 'restorative praxis' achieved through sharing experience and finding common ground – the interaction, conversation that 'brings the social into being' (Arendt, 1958). My active, repetitive stitching links to the rhythms of industrial production in these now empty or lost spaces and to the new rhythms of the continuously changing landscapes around these places.

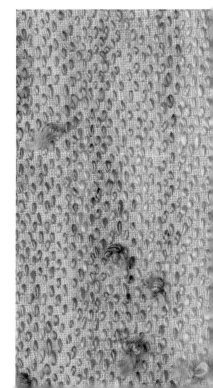

Above and right Lull *(2016–2017), detail. Recycled linen, silk thread dyed with found plant material, hand stitch.*

114

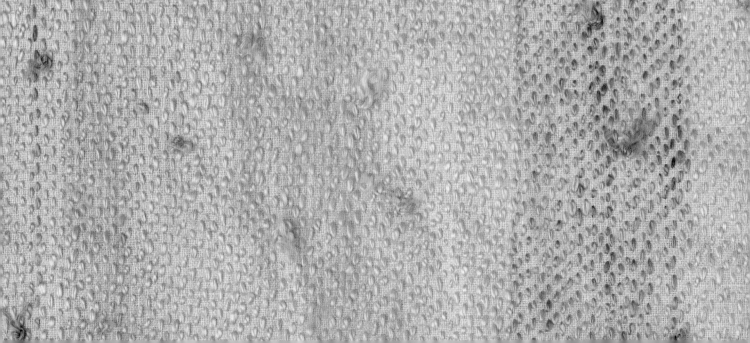

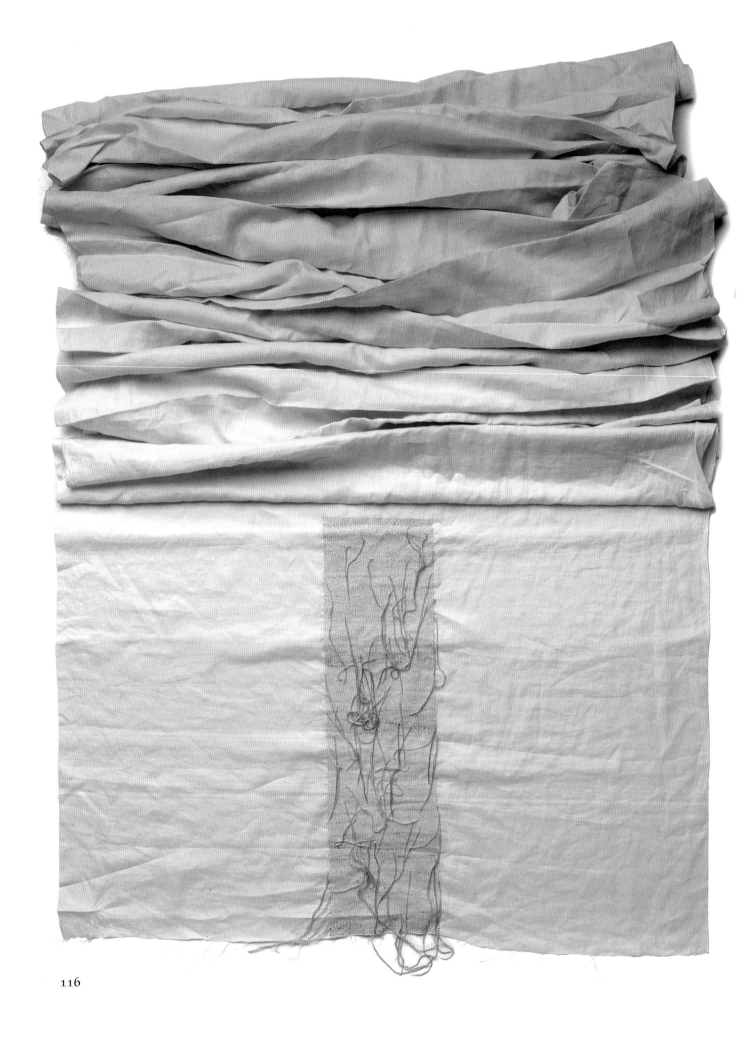

As I was writing the final parts of this book during a particularly bad spell of winter weather, floodwater affected the basement studio in my house. As a temporary measure we piled bags and boxes of work, fabrics, parts of community projects and exhibition props at one end of the room while the rest dried out. The messiness and many layers of my textile practice seemed evident in the stacks of stuff, but somewhere in the mess I also began to see the potential for adaptation and growth. Unravelling it all felt rather like the unravelling of ideas and concepts of what might make a resilient textile. A complex collection of evolving ideas, of making and unmaking, and thinking and having conversations through materials.

Opposite Lull *(2016–17). Recycled linen, silk thread dyed with found plant material, hand stitch. 91 × 350cm (36 × 138in).*

Postscript: together apart

I completed the manuscript for this book in late February 2020. One month later much of the world was in lockdown as a response to the pandemic caused by the novel coronavirus, Covid-19. Work and everyday life suddenly looked very different, and the types of community-based projects described in this book were halted as a social distancing requirement. Across the media I heard the word 'resilience' used time and again to describe the need for health systems, economies, communities, families and individuals to adapt to what was described as the 'new normal'. Textile projects usually work with people who gather together in the same space. They thrive through touch: the handle of fabrics and the sensation of working with them are shared in conversation. Fabrics and threads are passed around the table, the stitches and construction of items examined and held by all. The likelihood being that communities would have to behave very differently for the foreseeable future, I began to ask myself: what does a socially distant collaborative textile look like? As new kinds of community engagement began to emerge through online meetings, my laptop screen, a grid of colourful small squares, reminded me of a patchwork quilt.

The Bradford Covid-19 Stitch Journal Project

The Bradford Covid-19 Stitch Journal Project was my immediate response to this crisis and was supported by funding from the local council in Bradford, West Yorkshire, where I live. It offered an opportunity for a group to gather together in a different kind of community project. I sent out 30 packs of materials in the post and then organized online meetings where participants could explore their feelings about lockdown, then work at home on textile samples to communicate their experience using stitch. On signing up to take part, participants expressed a desire to make a record of this particular time. As one wrote to me, 'I am interested in finding ways to 'understand' this odd time and how I might respond in a creative way.'

As part of an offering of creative prompts, I asked participants to first think of a word that expressed something of their feelings about lockdown and then to stitch it. A wide range of responses emerged, from angry, subdued, unsettled and overwhelmed to grateful, grounded, growing and thankful.

Bradford Covid-19 Stitch
Journal *(May 2020).*
Stitched contributions
from participants, each
giving a word that
described their experience
of lockdown. Linen,
mixed threads.

The words were shared in our online meetings, with participants
open to describing their personal responses and the physical
experiences of stitching their feelings. Several commented on
the cathartic nature of the process, and also that it offered an
opportunity to reflect on wider themes, 'I found the act of stitching
very therapeutic … I also found that while stitching I thought about
the stories and experiences I'd heard from others in the group, and
found myself reflecting on the whole experience of not just this
project but the whole lockdown, the pandemic and my actions/
reactions in this time.'

The final piece of work for the project was a 20 x 20cm (8 x 8in)
square of linen stitched by each participant. The brief for this work
was fairly open: a stitched reflection of a personal experience
of lockdown. I suggested some simple prompts: 'Things you are
seeing, things you are hearing, things you are feeling.' I suggested
that text, simple stitches and patches of other fabric sewn to the

119

background linen could all be used to realize these ideas. Gathering again online to discuss the work the group had made as a response to these prompts was, for many, an emotional experience. The textile responses used everything from a stitched visualization of government data related to the UK Covid-19 mortality rate, to depictions of views from windows, to the inclusion of scraps of fabric from projects made with key workers' children still at school. Maps of local walks undertaken, a broken domestic textile mended and remade, a textile version of a drawing made by a grandchild, the grid of an empty diary page filled with stitches. A small luggage label of text accompanied each piece of work:

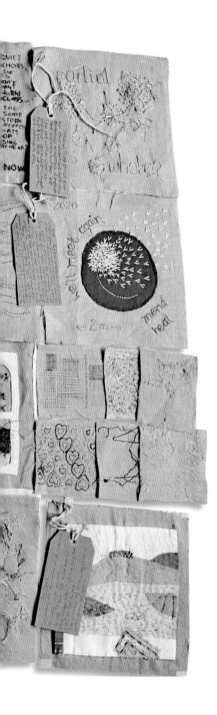

Home at the heart of a shrinking world. We walk the streets of our neighbourhood, by the river, through woodland and graveyard. Growing our garden, staying in touch with distant loved ones.

My home is represented by the circle at the heart of the stitching. Surrounding it, radiating out in a spiral are slogans, words and thoughts that have filled my head. Daily walks calm me and give me the space to reflect. I 'took my thread for a walk' meandering freely around the cloth but restrained by the size – like in lockdown – limited by how far I can go.

Our world feels dismantled, broken and in need of mending. This piece is made from fabric that has been taken apart and stitched back together. It's deliberately messy and unfinished, reflecting the uneasy and ongoing situation …

As I write this postscript the world is slowly emerging from lockdown, but the Covid-19 crisis and its impacts are far from over. The final completed squares of the Bradford Covid-19 Stitch Journal are starting to arrive in the post. Finally, I have an opportunity to look closely, touch the stitches, handle the texture of each square and read the short reflection that comes with each one. Each response is unique; part of our discussions as a group have shown that everyone is experiencing the crisis differently. However, the societal inequalities amplified by the crisis have been of concern to many. 'As I worked on this stitched map of my limited Covid world, I reflected on the contrast between my local environment and the much more challenging situations of many families in this city.'

The group has a plan to meet up physically to stitch together, once social distancing requirements allow. Despite the different quality of a community project in which everyone stays in their own homes, most participants have found the experience of meeting online positive in some respects: 'Because all of us connect … a lot of us have never met before at all and yet this is giving us space to talk through the stitching and through the unpicking of what we've stitched, we can talk about some quite important things and it gives us the space for that. So although there are things missing it is still a very special space.'

The experience of living through a global health crisis has allowed me to continue to consider my work with textiles and people in very different circumstances. Resilience, particularly as an idea that can encompass give and take, flexibility, and that offers an opportunity for reinvention, has never seemed more important.

Bradford Covid-19 Stitch Journal (June 2020). Contributions from participants. Linen, applique, stitch, with luggage labels containing personal reflections about each textile piece. Each 20 × 20cm (8 × 8in).

Notes

1 Anni Albers, *On Weaving*, p.59

2 Julia Bryan-Wilson, *Fray: Art and Textile Politics*, p.5

3 Samuel Jubb, *The History of the Shoddy-trade*, p.24

4 https://helencarnac.wordpress.com/2014/06/10/old-writing-of-mine/

5 Jennifer Higgie in *Duro Olowu: Making and Unmaking*, p.62

6 https://neweconomics.org/2008/10/five-ways-to-wellbeing-the-evidence

7 Annette B. Weiner and Jane Schneider (eds), *Cloth and Human Experience*, p.2

8 Nicky Gregson and Louise Crewe, *Second-hand Cultures*, p.145–6

9 Max Kozloff, 'The Poetics of Softness' in *Renderings: Critical Essays on a Century of Modern Art*, p.233

10 Winnicott, D.W., 'Transitional objects and transitional phenomena; a study of the first not-me possession', *The International Journal of Psychoanalysis*, 34 (1953), p.89–97

11 Elaine Showalter,'Piecing and Writing', in *The Textile Reader*, Ed. Jessica Hemmings (London: Berg, 2012), p.160

12 Albrecht, Glenn, 'The Age of Solastalgia', www.theconversation.com/the-age-of-solastalgia-8337

13 Nicholas Culpeper, *Complete Herbal*, p.227

14 Ibid, p.396

15 Joanna Macy and Chris Johnstone, *Active Hope*

16 Peter Dormer, *The Art of the Maker: Skill and its meaning in art, craft and design,* p.147

17 Diana Woolf, *Embroidery* magazine, September/October 2018, p.32

18 Beverly Gordon, *Textiles: The Whole Story,* p.10

19 Daniel Miller, *Stuff,* p.41

20 https://www.cheimread.com/exhibitions/louise-bourgeois_2

21 *Labour Leader*, 29 September 1917

22 Rebecca Solnit, *Wanderlust: A History of Walking*, p.xv

23 The *Yorkshire Observer*, Tuesday 28 May 1918

24 Correspondence and newscuttings on the Khaki Handicrafts Club, Bradford (War invalids rehabilitation centre) National Archives RAIL 491/854

25 https://www.theguardian.com/books/2017/jun/27/nick-laird-my-writing-day

26 Michael D. Jackson, *The Politics of Storytelling: Variations on a Theme by Hannah Arendt*, p.23

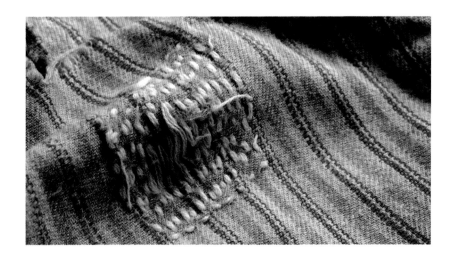

Darned tear on a salvaged cotton work shirt.

Bibliography

Albers, Anni, Nicholas Fox Weber, Manuel Cirauqui, T'ai Smith, *On Weaving*
  (Princeton: Princeton University Press, 2017 revised edition)
Albrecht, Glenn, 'The Age of Solastalgia', 2012. www.theconversation.com/the-age-of-solastalgia-8337
Arendt, Hannah, *The Human Condition* (Chicago: University of Chicago Press, 1958)
Bendadi, Samira and Mashid Mohadjerin, *Textile as Resistance* (Veurne: Hannibal Publishing, 2019)
Brooks, Andrew, *Clothing Poverty: The hidden world of fast fashion and second-hand clothes*
  (London: Zed Books, 2015)
Bryan-Wilson, Julia, *Fray: Art and Textile Politics* (Chicago: University of Chicago Press, 2017)
Chenciner, Robert, *Madder Red: A History of Luxury and Trade* (Abingdon: Routledge, 2000)
Constantine, Mildred and Laurel Reuter, *Whole Cloth* (New York: The Monacelli Press, 1987)
Corkhill, Betsan, *Knit for Health and Wellness* (Bath: FlatBear Publishing, 2014)
Dormer, Peter, *The Art of the Maker: Skill and Its Meaning in Art, Craft and Design*
  (London: Thames and Hudson, 1994)
Fletcher, Kate and Ingun Grimstad Klepp, *Opening up the Wardrobe: A methods book* (Norway: Novus, 2017)
Gale, Colin, and Jasbir Kaur, *The Textile Book* (Oxford: Berg, 2002)
Gauntlett, David, *Making is connecting: the social meaning of creativity, from DIY and knitting to YouTube and
  Web 2.0* (Cambridge: Polity Press, 2011)
Gordon, Beverly, *Textiles: the whole story: uses, meanings, significance* (London: Thames & Hudson, 2011)
Gregson, Nicky and Louise Crewe, *Second-hand Cultures* (Oxford: Berg, 2003)
Hemmings, Jessica (Ed.), *The Textile Reader* (London: Berg, 2012)
Jackson, Michael D., *The Politics of Storytelling: Variations on a Theme by Hannah Arendt*
  (Copenhagen: Museum Tusculanum Press, 2013)
Jubb, Samuel, *History of the Shoddy-trade* (London: Houlston and Wright, 1860)
Kettle, Alice, *Thread Bearing Witness* (Chichester: the artists agency, 2018)
Kozloff, Max, 'The Poetics of Softness' in *Renderings: Critical Essays on a Century of Modern Art*
  (London: Simon & Schuster, 1968), pp.223–35
Macy, Joanna and Chris Johnstone, *Active Hope* (Novato: New World Library, 2012)
Miller, Daniel, *Stuff* (Cambridge: Polity Press, 2011)
Oliver, Mary, *A Poetry Handbook* (San Diego: Harcourt Publishers Ltd, 1994)
Olowu, Duro, *Making and Unmaking* (London: Riding House and Camden Arts Centre, 2016)
Paine, Sheila, *Embroidered Textiles: A World Guide to Traditional Patterns* (London: Thames and Hudson, 1990)
Richmond, Vivienne, *Clothing the poor in nineteenth-century England*
  (Cambridge: Cambridge University Press, 2013)
Schneider, Jane and Annette Weiner, *Cloth and Human Experience*
  (Washington: Smithsonian Institution Press, 1989)
Sennett, Richard, *Together: The Rituals, Pleasures and Politics of Co-operation* (London: Penguin, 2013)
Snook, Barbara, *Embroidery Stitches* (London: Batsford, 1963)
Solnit, Rebecca, *Wanderlust: A History of Walking* (London: Penguin, 2001)
Wilson, Geoff, *Community Resilience and Environmental Transitions* (Abingdon: Routledge, 2012)
Winnicott, D.W., 'Transitional objects and transitional phenomena; a study of the first not-me possession'
  in *The International Journal of Psychoanalysis,* 34, 89–97 (1953)

Contributors' websites

Angela Maddock **www.angela-maddock.com**
Bridget Harvey **www.bridgetharvey.co.uk**
Raisa Kabir **lids-sewn-shut.typepad.com**
Amy Meissner **www.amymeissner.com**
Willemien de Villiers **www.willemiendevilliers.co.za**
Alice Kettle **www.alicekettle.co.uk**
Lynn Setterington **www.lynnsetterington.co.uk**
Claire Wellesley-Smith **www.clairewellesleysmith.co.uk**
Ruth Singer **www.ruthsinger.com**

Acknowledgements

I would like to thank the following:

Joy Hart and all at Hive
Shamim Akhtar, Roshni Ghar and all at the Sukoon-e-Dil group, Keighley
Worn Stories stitchers and researchers and Jennie Kiff, project consultant
National Lottery Heritage Fund
Arts Council England
Bradford Metropolitan District Council and participants in the Bradford Covid-19 Stitch Journal Project
George Revill
The Open University
Debs Greensill
Elly Maynard
June Hill
Gawthorpe Textiles Collection
Community Works project, Bradford
Workshop attendees for all your insight and helpful feedback
Kristy Richardson, Nicola Newman and all at Batsford for supporting this book
Michael Wicks for the wonderful photography

Community participants' quotes are used with permission.

This book is for Btje.

Patched and pieced sample in progress, using hand-dyed and vintage fabrics. For instructions see page 36.

Picture credits

All photographs by Michael Wicks except for the following: pages 12, 23, 44, 46, 49, 62 (bottom), 65, 96, 97, 98, 119, 120 Claire Wellesley-Smith; 5, 43, 52, 53, 54, 62 (top) Claire Wellesley-Smith/Hive; 28 Brian Adams; 38, 39 Lynn Setterington; 55, 56 Huw Maddock; 66 Bart De Nil; 72 David Stelfox; 73 Bridget Harvey; 80 Raisa Kabir and Angela Dennis; 82–85 Michael Pollard (image courtesy of Alice Kettle and Candida Stevens Gallery); 90 Paul Lapsley; 102 Two Temple Place; 103 Leeds University Library Special Collections (ITC 1835); 104 Etienne De Villiers.

Contributing artists to *Sky* (2018), pages 82–83: Amran Abdi Mohamed, Iqra Abdi Mohamed, Idil Abdi Mohamud, Ayantu Abdii, Abdirahman, Abdi Muse, Farhia Ahmed Ali, Bile Ali Aden, Alias Aliye Musa Aliye, Gutu Habib, Monica Hamakami, Isha HassanBare, Nawad Hersi Duale, Muno Idiris Mohamed, Mohamed Ahmed Mezan Ismail, Tajura Lamiso Gatiso, Khadar Mohamud Ismail, Sahra Mohamud Ismail, Amran Mohamud Ismail, Fartun Umar Jimale. All with Refugee Action and working with artists Jenny Eden and Richard Harris; Julie Firman, Victoria Hartley, Louise Jung and Saamiullah Khan. Interpreters: Ramadan Ahmed, Abas El Janabi and Mohamed Hirey.

Contributing artists to *Ground* (2018) and *Sea* (2017), pages 84–85: Pikpa/Lesvos Solidarity, Ahmad Ali, Somaya Hossaini, Yakob and many other residents at a Calais refugee camp working with Suzanne Partridge; Nahomie Bukasa, Sahira Khan and Ai Ling with Linda Leroy at the Helen Bamber Foundation; Nisrin Albyrouty, Khouloud Alkurd, Heba Almnini, Heidi Ambruster, Marwa Ammar, Amal Ayoubi, Stella Charman, Susan Colverson, Jenny Cuffe, Lama Hamami, Miriam Jones, Asmaa Kamar Aldin, Ruth le Mesurier, Vanessa Rolf, Samar Sobeih, Chaymae Yousfi and many children from English Chat Winchester; Farhia Ahmed Ali, Nawad Hersi Duale, Amran Mohamud Ismail with Refugee Action working with artists Jenny Eden and Richard Harris; Julie Firman, Victoria Hartley, Louise Jung, Susan Kamara, Saamiullah Khan.

Stockists

Fabrics

Offset Warehouse
www.offsetwarehouse.com
Eco fabrics and haberdashery including peace silk.

Greenfibres
www.greenfibres.com
Organic and sustainable fabric, wadding and sewing threads.

Threads

Airedale Yarns
www.airedaleyarns.co.uk
Large selection of yarns and threads for dyeing.

Needles

John James
www.jjneedles.com

Dyes

Wild Colours
www.wildcolours.co.uk
Natural dyestuffs and mordants.

The Textile Society

www.textilesociety.org.uk
The society holds two antique textiles fairs every year in the UK – a great source of inspiration and somewhere to purchase unusual secondhand materials from all over the world.

Simple running stitches embedded in indigo-dyed and vintage fabrics.

Index